Prayers *for the* Common Good

Prayers

for the

Common

Good

Edited by A. Jean Lesher

The Pilgrim Press
Cleveland, Ohio

The Pilgrim Press, Cleveland, Ohio 44115

Printed in Hong Kong on acid-free paper

03 02 01 00 99 98 5 4 3 2 1

Library of Congress Cataloging-in-Publication Data

Prayers for the common good / edited by A. Jean Lesher.
p. cm.
Includes index.
ISBN 0-8298-1248-2 (alk. paper)
1. Prayers. 2. Meditations. 3. Common good—Prayer-books and devotions—English. I. Lesher, A. Jean.
BL560.P725 1998
291.4'32—dc21 97-47076
CIP

To my dearest Bill

and

in memory of

Jan Gallagher

Contents

Acknowledgments

The Pilgrim Press maintains a commendable policy that its published texts use inclusive language when referring to people and to belief in a genderless God. Some of the readings within this book have been altered as marked and where permitted by copyright holders to reflect this policy. Some copyright holders have not permitted such changes and so the original language is retained. Certain quotations from sacred texts of other religions that use masculine language for God and people have been retained out of respect for their beliefs and traditions. Such respect is a requirement, I believe, to maintain meaningful conversations among peoples of differing religions. I hope soon we will have new translations of sacred texts to reflect and even help bring about changes in the future regarding the equality of women and the essential nature of deities in all religions.

I am deeply grateful to those who have supported my work in collecting readings for this text in recent years. My husband, Bill, and I have been dedicated to several causes incorporated in the concept of the common good over the many years of our life together, including several facets of civil rights, race relations, ecumenism, and international understanding. He is a wonderful companion and support in this ongoing journey. My friend Aimee Horton, director of the Lindeman Center for democratic social change, is a constant source of inspiration, as are so many others who devote their lives to serving others in public policy and social service efforts and for whom we thank God daily.

I want to express public appreciation to those persons who took time to review my manuscript and provide most helpful comments: Don Benedict, Linda-Marie Delloff, Inagrace Dietrich, Mary Nelson, Alice Peppler, Bill Lesher, and Wendy Tweeten. I also am grateful to my editor at the Pilgrim Press, Tim Staveteig, for his support and encouragement.

Introduction

If we find our hearts, after all, very barren, and hardly know how to frame a prayer before God of ourselves, it has been oftentimes useful to take a book in our hand, wherein are contained some spiritual meditations in a petitionary form, some devout reflections, or excellent patterns of prayer.

—Sir Isaac Watts, 1674–1748

This collection of readings as prayers began several years ago. It came from a desire to find spiritual resources for facing daily reminders of powerful forces that threaten to destroy our common well-being in our national and international living together.

I am troubled by what appear to be increasing levels of antagonism and disregard for others in hate crimes and family violence and an irrational hostility toward institutions of our society, especially government, which we have elected to provide stability and safety. In our city, I see more poverty at the same time that there is more wealth than a few years ago. Both at home and abroad there continues to be a callous exploitation of the environment that affects all living species. We are all aware, too, that with contemporary technologies, we have a greater capacity to destroy whole nations and the world than ever before, slowly through environmental degradations or quickly in nuclear annihilation should regional conflicts or terrorism spread.

In 1993, heads of the National Council of Churches, the U.S. Catholic Conference, and the Synagogue Council of America issued "A Call to the Common Ground for the Common Good." The call affirmed "the common ground of faith in one holy and loving God" and judged "this moment, especially, to be filled with great promise for . . . renewal of the national bond which extends to every person in our land . . ." and to "quicken our responsiveness not only to our budget deficits but more profoundly to our growing social deficits. It is these that have most dramatically rent the fabric of life for our people."

How do people of faith respond to repeated experiences and reports of human sinfulness—of alienation from one another, of disobedience to all the ethics of world religions? Like people of good will everywhere, we do what we can to relieve problems in our families and among our neighbors, and we join and contribute to organizations and movements that serve the common good both here and in relations with other countries and peoples. And, as people have done through the ages, we pray—a lot. All of us are concerned about the evils we see and hear about daily. We need reminders that God is with us, that our efforts to serve are blessed, and that we can, with God's help, affect our futures as individuals and nations.

Many of the readings in this collection can be called "prayers" only if you understand praying, as I do, to be almost anything—music, art, stories, people, sights, experiences, etc.—that causes one to think about God or spiritual matters. The readings might be called meditations or reflections or even "thoughts," as well. I like what Joseph Cardinal Bernardin said shortly before his death in 1996: "Through prayer I become grounded in the Lord, which has a positive effect on the way I view the events of my life and make decisions." I also like what novelist Victor Hugo said: "Certain thoughts are prayers. There are moments when, whatever be the attitude of the body, the soul is on its knees."

When I read something thought-provoking, I consider such thoughts a religious experience. I marvel at some new invention described in a magazine or empathize with parents in a photograph whose children are suffering or I admire a great achievement. Often these thoughts turn into a prayer for the good use of an invention or the comfort of the parents or the well-being of an achiever. The readings in this collection, insofar as they are thought-provoking, can also be prayer-provoking.

Selections for this collection came from hundreds of sources in different books, worship programs, newspapers, and magazines. From about two thousand possibilities, the final ones were chosen using several criteria: The readings should, if possible, be by sources familiar to people who know religious literature; they should come from the past and the present and from women and men of differing races and cultures; they should be thought-provoking; they should be varied in length and genre, a mixture of poems, prose, documents, and worship forms to maintain interest; and they should include some examples from other faith traditions. The overall intent is for readers to feel spiritually nourished, strengthened, and hopeful about their own efforts to serve the common good.

The readings are divided into four parts to follow a quasiliturgical approach to the subject of the common good. The title of the first section, "Then I Saw a New Heaven and a New Earth: The Vision for the Common Good," contains a quotation from the book of Revelation 21:1. Contextual information is provided with each reading in the sections to give a perspective on the content. One selection contains a definition of the common good from the National Conference of Catholic Bishops: "the sum of those conditions of social life which allow social groups and their individual members relatively thorough and ready access to their own fulfillment." This prosaic wording is fleshed out in subsequent readings in more poetic language that expresses the hopes and dreams of believers who see the common good as a holy commandment for all times and places.

The second part is entitled "Forgive Us Our Trespasses: The Need for Mercy." Most of us are aware of our failings as individuals and citizens to meet the challenges of social, economic, cultural, and political forces that prevent realization of our visions and dreams. Even the status quo in our nation and world is threatened. Our own families and friends may be victims of crime or economic dislocation or suffering from the lack of adequate health care. We can ask forgiveness for our sins of commission and omission in these situations and we can expect mercy from a God whose nature is love.

The heart of the concept of the common good is service to others, as the third part title indicates: "Love Your Neighbor As Yourself: The Call to Care for Others." This is the longest section. Here ancient and contemporary passages remind us of our responsibilities. These are embodied not only in sacred writings of many faiths but also in the documents of national and world bodies—the U.S. constitution, the UN charter, and declarations by many secular organizations. These documents are examples of God at work in the world and through history, where people of faith can publicly express their highest aspirations for the well-being of this nation and planet. In my research, I found that use of the term "human rights" has arisen only since the Second World War and the formation of the United Nations. The concept is now an international standard that leaders of all nations must consider and be judged by even as some reject it.

The fourth and final part, "So That You Will Be a Blessing: Gratitude for God's Gifts," is one of thanksgiving for all God has given us and of hope for what may be. The title quotation, "So That You Will Be a Blessing," is from Genesis 12:1–3, where God says to Abraham: "Go from your country and . . . I will bless you, and make your name great, so that you will be a blessing . . . and in you all the families of the earth shall be blessed." The readings praise God for all of creation, including the gift of life itself. God's gifts in the world of nature and in our sisters and brothers in the faith have always been an inspiration for renewal and hope. With such resources we need not be discouraged and wearied of well-doing, and we can know that we are blessed so that we may be a blessing to others.

The sequence of readings within each section is intended to provide a variety of sources and literary genres and to cluster some ideas that segue from one to another. My assumption is that most readers will choose selections to read as a mood strikes rather than read from beginning to end. My hope is that this collection will be a continuing resource for private and for group devotions and will also provide quotations and ideas for public speakers.

As you meditate on the passages that follow, I hope you also will experience epiphanies of insight, reassurance, renewal, and hope from them. The images and words, from ancient to contemporary writers of many lands and cultures, can help us sense the web of kinship—back and forth and up and down—that attests to the unity of all before God.

Prayer is as complex and as simple as the people who use this means to commune with a loving and a just God. Prayer also can enable us to commune with others, near and far, and give us strength to continue lives of service for a more humane nation and world.

I

"Then I Saw a New Heaven and a New Earth"

The Vision for the Common Good

The starting point for a better world is the belief that it is possible. Civilization begins in the imagination. The wild dream is the first step to reality. It is the direction-finder by which people locate higher goals and discern their highest selves.

—Norman Cousins, 1912–1990

From earliest recorded times, prophets and seers, shamans and poets have described what was required of believers to live lives of righteousness or goodness. Justice and charity are basic elements of the visions that have persisted through the ages and become embodied in secular documents for nations and peoples.

Many of us grew up hearing the proverb from the King James Version of the Bible: "Where there is no vision, the people perish" (Proverbs 29:18a). This wording persists with us because we believe it to be true even though more recent translations have a slightly different meaning: "Where there is no prophecy, the people cast off restraint" (NRSV). Both wordings, however, give an image of the grave social consequences, even chaos, that would result if we do not retain prophetic visions of what our society should or can become. A common vision of our goals is part of the "social contract" essential for the common good. The passages that follow present aspects of the visions we have had and still have.

"With what shall I come before the Lord,
and bow myself before God on high?
Shall I come before him with burnt offerings,
with calves a year old?
Will the Lord be pleased with thousands of rams,
with ten thousands of rivers of oil?
Shall I give my firstborn for my transgression,
the fruit of my body for the sin of my soul?"

He has told you, O mortal, what is good;
and what does the Lord require of you
but to do justice,
and to love kindness,
and to walk humbly with your God?

—*Micah 6:6–8*

~

Now the onely way . . . to provide for our posterity is to followe the Counsell of Micah, to doe Justly, to love mercy, to walke humbly with our God.

For this end, wee must be knitt together in this worke as one, wee must entertaine each other in Affeccion, wee must be willing to abridge our selves of our superfluities, for the supply of others necessities, wee must uphold a familiar Commerce together in all meeknes, gentlenes, patience and liberallity, wee must delight in each other, make others Condicions our owne, rejoyce together, mourne together, labour and suffer together, allwayes haveing before our eyes our Commission and Community in the worke, our Community as members of the same body, soe shall wee keepe the unitie of the spirit in the bond of peace, the Lord will be our God and delight to dwell among us and will commaund a blessing upon us in all our wayes, soe that wee shall see much more of godly wisdome, power, goodnes and truthe than formerly wee have beene acquainted with. . . .

And to shutt upp this discourse with that exhortacion of Moses, that faithfull servant of the Lord in his last farewell to Isreall, Deut. 30. Beloved there is now sett before us life, and good, deathe and evill in that wee are Commaunded this day to love the Lord our God, and to love one another, to walke in Gods wayes and to keepe Gods Commaundements and Ordinance, and lawes, and the Articles of our Covenant that wee may live and be multiplied, and that the Lord our God may blesse us in the land whither we goe to possesse it: But if our heartes shall turne away soe that wee will not obey, but shall be seduced and worship . . . other Gods, our pleasures, and proffitts, and serve them; it is propounded unto us this day, wee shall surely perishe out of the good Land whither wee passe over this vast Sea to possesse it;

Therefore lett us choose life, that wee,
and our Seede, may live;
by obeyeing Gods voyce, and cleaveing to God,
who is our life, and our prosperity.

—*John Winthrop, 1588–1649;* alt.

This sermon, "A Modell of Christian Charity," was preached by Winthrop, the first governor of the Massachusetts Bay Colony, on board ship in 1630 even before the settlers landed in the New World. In establishing a consciousness of social obligation, this sermon has become an important political document in U.S. history.

~

In holy and infinite love,
God has created us
for community
and has called us
to covenants of justice
and the common good.

The word of God
is addressed to communities,
to cities, to nations,
to the whole family of nations,
so that all Earth's peoples
may become one people.

The will of God
is forsaken whenever a nation
fails to nurture and sustain
the dignity and rights
of all its people.

—*National Council of the Churches of Christ, USA*
Synagogue Council of America
United States Catholic Conference

This reading is from "A Call to the Common Ground for the Common Good" issued June 8, 1993, by the three religious bodies in response to constituency concerns about the social well-being of American society.

~

Vatican II described the common good as "the sum of those conditions of social life which allow social groups and their individual members relatively thorough and ready access to their own fulfillment."[1] These conditions include the rights to fulfillment of material needs, a guarantee of fundamental freedoms, and the protection of relationships that are essential to participation in the life of society.[2] These rights are bestowed on human beings by God and grounded in the nature and dignity of human persons. They are not created by society. Indeed society has a duty to secure and protect them.[3]

—*National Conference of Catholic Bishops, 1997*

From the pastoral letter "Economic Justice for All: Catholic Social Teaching and the U.S. Economy," first distributed in 1986 and updated in 1997. The footnotes for sources may be found in the Copyright Acknowledgments.

~

Grant, Almighty God, that all who confess your Name may be united in your truth, live together in your love, and reveal your glory in the world.
Silence
Lord, in your mercy.
Hear our prayer.
Guide the people of this land, and of all the nations, in the ways of justice and peace; that we may honor one another and serve the common good.
Silence
Lord, in your mercy.
Hear our prayer.
Give us all a reverence for the earth as your own creation, that we may use its resources rightly in the service of others and to your honor and glory.

Silence
Lord, in your mercy.
Hear our prayer.
Bless all whose lives are closely linked with ours, and grant that we may serve Christ in them, and love one another as he loves us.
Silence
Lord, in your mercy.
Hear our prayer.

—*The Book of Common Prayer*

The Book of Common Prayer dates from the reign of Henry VIII (d.1547) when the Church of England became the official religion. This selection, "Prayer of the People (Form IV)," is from its edition published in 1979.

~

Social welfare policy in the United States must be fundamentally reformed and modernized. Economic, demographic, and social conditions have changed, but our social policies have not adapted to these changes. . . .

Our basic premise is that we must stop pitting one group against another in the struggle to improve social policy. We believe that if an unmet need is effectively addressed, we all benefit, not just those who have that need at that particular time. Similarly, if that need is neglected and problems fester, we all pay, and we usually pay more by delaying. It is essential that we improve economic opportunities and strengthen social protections for our most vulnerable citizens. These themes are not antithetical but complementary, and they cut across all age groups. . . .

Each and every one of us has a stake in providing infants and young children, wherever they may live, the nutrition and emotional nurturing that allow them a decent start in life, both because it is right and because if we don't, they may burden us for decades with the costs of illness, dependency, and crime. All of us have a stake in helping adolescents and young adults make a successful transition from school to the increasingly demanding work force of the information age. All have an interest in retraining workers who are left behind by a changing economy so they will not be condemned to unproductive, dependent lives. And all can find personal reassurance in providing the elderly with freedom from the fear that an infirmity will devastate not only their health but also their family's financial and emotional underpinnings.

Such practical considerations argue strongly for the importance of dealing with the social deficit; the panel finds this effort to be not only right but also politically realistic. At the same time, there is a powerful moral reason to pursue the task. Social welfare policy is properly the concern of all Americans, not just because all may benefit from improving it but because improving it is the right thing to do. The moral integrity of our society depends in no small measure upon our ability to unite behind this belief.

—*The Ford Foundation*

The Ford Foundation's Project on Social Welfare and the American Future completed its research and published its findings in a report entitled *The Common Good* in 1989. This selection is an excerpt from the first chapter, "Reexamining Our Social Welfare System."

~

Almighty God; We make our earnest prayer that Thou wilt keep the United States in Thy Holy protection; and Thou wilt incline the hearts of the Citizens to cultivate a spirit of subordination and obedience to Government; and entertain an affection and love for one another and for all Citizens of the United States at large, and particularly for those who have served in the Field.

And finally that Thou wilt most graciously be pleased to dispose us all to do justice, to love mercy, and to demean ourselves with that Charity, humility, and pacific temper of mind which were the Characteristics of the Divine Author of our blessed Religion, and without a humble imitation of whose example in these things we can never hope to be a happy nation.

Grant our supplication, we beseech Thee, in the Name of Jesus Christ. Amen.

—*General George Washington, 1732–1799;* alt.

This prayer is the concluding paragraph in Washington's farewell circular letter sent in 1783 to the governors of the thirteen states from his military headquarters in Newburgh, New York.

~

Centuries used to divide the world into their friends and foes. No longer. The foes now are universal—poverty, famine, religious radicalization, desertification, drugs, proliferation of nuclear weapons, ecological devastation. They threaten all nations, just as science and information are the potential friends of all nations.

Classical diplomacy and strategy were aimed at identifying enemies and confronting them. Now they have to identify dangers, global or local, and tackle them before they become disasters. . . .

Science must be learned; it cannot be conquered. An army that can occupy knowledge has yet to be built. And that is why armies of occupation are a thing of the past. Indeed, even for defensive purposes, a country cannot rely on its army alone. Territorial frontiers are no obstacle to ballistic missiles, and no weapon can shield from a nuclear device. Today, therefore, the battle for survival must be based on political wisdom and moral vision no less than on military might.

—*Shimon Peres*

As foreign minister in the government of Yitzhak Rabin, Peres helped negotiate a peace agreement with the Palestine Liberation Organization, an achievement that brought him, Yasser Arafat, and Rabin the 1994 Nobel Peace Prize. This excerpt is from his acceptance speech.

~

I say to you today, my friends, that in spite of the difficulties and frustrations of the moment, I still have a dream. It is a dream deeply rooted in the American dream.

I have a dream that one day this nation will rise up and live out the true meaning of its creed: "We hold these truths to be self-evident: that all men are created equal."

I have a dream that one day on the red hills of Georgia the sons of former slaves and the sons of former slaveowners will be able to sit down together at a table of brotherhood.

I have a dream that one day even the state of Mississippi, a desert state, sweltering with the heat of injustice and oppression, will be transformed into an oasis of freedom and justice.

I have a dream that my four children will one day live in a nation where they will not be judged by the color of their skin but by the content of their character.

I have a dream today.

I have a dream that one day the state of Alabama, whose governor's lips are presently dripping with the words of interposition and nullification, will be transformed into a situation where little black boys and black girls will be able to join hands with little white boys and white girls and walk together as sisters and brothers.

I have a dream today.

I have a dream that one day every valley shall be exalted, every hill and mountain shall be made low, the rough places will be made plain, and the crooked places will be made straight, and the glory of the Lord shall be revealed, and all flesh shall see it together.

This is our hope. This is the faith with which I return to the South. With this faith we will be able to hew out of the mountain of despair a stone of hope. With this faith we will be able to transform the jangling discords of our nation into a beautiful symphony of brotherhood. With this faith we will be able to work together, to pray together, to struggle together, to go to jail together, to stand up for freedom together, knowing that we will be free one day.

This will be the day when all of God's children will be able to sing with a new meaning, "My country, 'tis of thee, sweet land of liberty, of thee I sing. Land where my fathers died, land of the pilgrim's pride, from every mountainside, let freedom ring."

And if America is to be a great nation this must become true. So let freedom ring from the prodigious hilltops of New Hampshire. Let freedom ring from the mighty mountains of New York. Let freedom ring from the heightening Alleghenies of Pennsylvania! Let freedom ring from the snowcapped Rockies of Colorado! Let freedom ring from the curvaceous peaks of California!

But not only that; let freedom ring from Stone Mountain of Georgia! Let freedom ring from Lookout Mountain of Tennessee!

Let freedom ring from every hill and every molehill of Mississippi. From every mountainside, let freedom ring.

When we let freedom ring, when we let it ring from every village and every hamlet, from every state and every city, we will be able to speed up that day when all of God's children, black men and white men, Jews and Gentiles, Protestants and Catholics, will be able to join hands and sing in the words of the old Negro spiritual, "Free at last! free at last! thank God Almighty, we are free at last!"

—Martin Luther King Jr., 1928–1968

August 28, 1963, was the date of the historic civil rights March on Washington where King made his impassioned "I Have a Dream" speech. It is credited with rallying support for crucial congressional legislation in support of civil rights.

~

And then all that has divided us will merge
And then compassion will be wedded to power
And then softness will come to a world
that is harsh and unkind

And then both men and women will be gentle
And then both women and men will be strong
And then no person
will be subject to another's will
And then all will be rich and free and varied
And then the greed of some
will give way to the needs of many
And then all will share equally
in the earth's abundance
And then all will care
for the sick and the weak and the old
And then all will nourish the young
And then all will cherish life's creatures
And then all will live
in harmony with each other and the earth.
And then everywhere
will be called Eden once again.

—*Judy Chicago*

Judy Chicago's unique artistic installation of ceramic and fabric place settings entitled "The Dinner Party," 1979, was dedicated to famous women in history. This poem was quoted in *Prayers for All People,* edited by Mary Ford-Grabowsky, 1995.

~

One of the interesting things that has happened to the understanding of salvation today is that, in a world of diversity and change, people feel free to use a variety of definitions of salvation. In the search for meaning every religion and ideology is explored for its offer of liberation, wholeness, and blessing. There is a growing awareness of the wholeness of human beings in their body, mind, and spirit and in their social relationships in today's world. For some this has led to a renewed stress on shalom as a gift of total wholeness and well-being in community.

The search for peace in a wartorn world where each new outbreak of fighting brings not only untold suffering but the threat of total destruction has led others to speak of *shalom* as the symbol of peace and harmony for which they long and work. Others see *shalom* as an expression of wholeness and harmony between humanity and the environment which is being destroyed by a technological society.

—*Letty M. Russell*

Russell is one of the first of the feminist theologians to describe new understandings of traditional theology incorporating more emphasis on social concerns. This excerpt is from her book *Human Liberation in a Feminist Perspective,* 1974.

~

When the Grand course was pursued,
a public and common spirit ruled all under the sky;
they chose people of talents, virtue and ability;
their words were sincere, and what they cultivated
    was harmony.
Thus people did not love their parents only,
nor treat as children only their own.
An effective provision was secured for the aged
    till their death,
employment for the able-bodied,
and the means of growing up to the young.
They showed kindness and compassion to widows/ers,

orphans, childless people, and those who were disabled by
disease, so that they were all sufficiently maintained.
Males had their proper work, and females had their homes.
[They accumulated] articles [of value],
disliking that they should be thrown away upon the ground,
but not wishing to keep them for their own gratification.
[They labored] with their strength,
disliking that it should not be exerted,
but not exerting it [only] with a view to their
own advantage.
In this way [selfish] scheming was repressed
and found no development.
Robbers, filchers and rebellious traitors did not show
themselves, and hence the outer doors remained open,
and were not shut.
This was [the period of] what we call the Grand Union.

—*Confucius, 551–479* B.C.E.

Chinese philosopher and reformer Confucius is also known as K'ung Fu-Tzu. His writings have been compiled into the "Analects." The translator of this work, known as "The Grand Union," is J. Legge.

~

To reflect on the basis of the historical praxis of liberation is to reflect in the light of the future which is believed in and hoped for. It is to reflect with a view to action which transforms the present. But it does not mean doing this from an armchair; rather it means sinking roots where the pulse of history is beating at this moment and illuminating history with the Word of the [God] of history. . . .

It is for all these reasons that the theology of liberation offers us not so much a new theme for reflection as a *new way* to do theology. Theology as critical reflection on historical praxis is a liberating theology, a theology of the liberating transformation of the history of [humankind] and also therefore that part of [humankind]—gathered into *ecclesia*—which openly confesses Christ. This is a theology which does not stop with reflecting on the world, but rather tries to be part of the process through which the world is transformed. It is a theology which is open—in the protest against trampled human dignity, in the struggle against the plunder of the vast majority of people, in liberating love, and in the building of a new, just, and fraternal society—to the gift of the Kingdom of God.

—*Gustavo Gutiérrez;* alt.

Peruvian Gutiérrez is the author of *A Theology of Liberation: History, Politics, and Salvation,* 1973, from which this selection is taken.

~

O God, grant us a vision of this city, fair as it may be; a city of justice, where none shall prey upon the other; a city of plenty, where vice and poverty shall cease to fester; a city of brotherhood, where success is founded on service, and honor is given to nobleness alone; a city of peace, where order shall not rest on force, but on the love of all for each and all. Amen.

—*Walter Rauschenbusch, 1861–1918*

A Baptist clergyperson, educator, and writer, Rauschenbusch is best known for his leadership in "the social gospel" movement of the late nineteenth and early twentieth centuries in support of practical social service rather than just individual salvation.

~

All human beings are born free and equal in dignity and rights. They are endowed with reason and conscience and should act towards one another in a spirit of [kinship].

Everyone is entitled to all the rights and freedoms set forth in this Declaration, without distinction of any kind, such as race, colour, sex, language, religion, political or other opinion, national or social origin, property, birth or other status. Furthermore, no distinction shall be made on the basis of the political, jurisdictional or international status of the country or territory to which a person belongs, whether it be independent, trust, non-self-governing or under any other . . . sovereignty.

No one shall be subjected to torture or cruel, inhuman or degrading treatment or punishment.

All are equal before the law and are entitled without any discrimination to equal protection of the law. All are entitled to equal protection against any discrimination in violation of this Declaration and against any incitement to such discrimination.

Everyone charged with a penal offence has the right to be presumed innocent until proved guilty according to law in a public trial at which [one] has had all the guarantees necessary for [one's] defense. . . .

Everyone has the right to freedom of movement and residence within the borders of each state.

Everyone has the right to leave any country, including [one's] own, and return to [one's] country.

Everyone has the right to seek and to enjoy in other countries asylum from persecution. . . .

Everyone has the right to a nationality.

No one shall be arbitrarily deprived of [one's] nationality or denied the right to change [one's] nationality.

Men and women of full age, without any limitation due to race, nationality or religion, have the right to marry and to found a family. They are entitled to equal rights as to marriage, during marriage and at its dissolution.

Marriage shall be entered into only with the free and full consent of the intending spouses.

—*From the United Nations Universal Declaration of Human Rights, 1948;* alt.

The term "human rights" only came into common use after World War II, when the UN Universal Declaration was adopted. Scholars trace the concept to the Hebrew Bible.

~

If we are to teach real peace in this world and if we are to carry on a real war against war, we shall have to begin with children; and if they will grow up in their natural innocence, we won't have to struggle; we won't have to pass fruitless, idle resolutions, but we shall go from love to love and peace to peace, until at last all the corners of the world are covered with that peace and love for which, consciously or unconsciously, the whole world is hungering.

—*Mahatma Mohandas Gandhi, 1869–1948*

World leader for nonviolent social change on behalf of the common good for all people, Gandhi was the inspiration for Martin Luther

King Jr.'s nonviolent protests. This passage is from a speech Gandhi gave in India in November 1931.

~

The goal of [humankind] is not progress toward a final stage of perfection; it is the creation of what is possible for [us] in each particular state of history; and it is the struggle against the forces of evil, old ones and new ones, which arise in each period in a different way.

There will be victories as well as defeats in these struggles. There will be progress and regressions. But every victory, every particular progress from injustice to more justice, from suffering to more happiness, from hostility to more peace, from separation to more unity anywhere [among us], is a manifestation of the eternal in time and space. It is, in the language of the [writers] of the Old and the New Testaments, the coming of the Kingdom of God. For the Kingdom of God does not come in one dramatic event sometime in the future. It is coming here and now in every act of love, in every manifestation of truth, in every moment of joy, in every experience of the holy.

The hope of the Kingdom of God is not the expectation of a perfect stage at the end of history, in which only a few, in comparison with innumerable [generations], would participate, and the unimaginable amount of misery of all past generations would not be compensated. And it might even be that those who would live in it, as "blessed animals," would long for the struggles, the victories and the defeats of the past. No! The hope of [humankind] lies in the here and now, whenever the eternal appeals in time and history. This hope is justified; for there is always a presence and a beginning of what is seriously hoped for.

—*Paul Tillich, 1886–1965;* alt.

Theologian Paul Tillich first preached these words in a sermon at Harvard's Memorial Church in March 1965.

~

In the future days, which we seek to make secure, we look forward to a world founded upon four essential human freedoms.

The first is freedom of speech and expression—everywhere in the world.

The second is freedom of people to worship God in their own way—everywhere in the world.

The third is freedom from want—which, translated into world terms, means economic understandings which will secure to every nation a healthy peacetime life for its inhabitants—everywhere in the world.

The fourth is freedom from fear—which, translated into world terms, means a world-wide reduction of armaments to such a point and in such a thorough fashion that no nation will be in a position to commit an act of physical aggression against any neighbor—anywhere in the world.

That is no vision of a distant millennium. It is a definite basis for a kind of world attainable in our own time and generation. That kind of world is the very antithesis of the so-called new order of tyranny which the dictators seek to create with the crash of a bomb.

To that new order we oppose the greater conception—the moral order. A good society is able to face schemes of world domination and foreign revolutions alike without fear.

Since the beginning of our American history, we have been engaged in change—in a perpetual peaceful revolution—a revolution which goes on steadily, quietly adjusting itself to changing conditions—without the concentration camp or the quick-lime in the ditch. The world order which we seek is the cooperation of free countries, working together in a friendly, civilized society.

This nation has placed its destiny in the hands and heads and hearts of its millions of free men and women; and its faith in freedom under the guidance of God. Freedom means the supremacy of human rights everywhere. Our support goes to those who struggle to gain those rights or keep them. Our strength is our unity of purpose.

To that high concept there can be no end save victory.

—*Franklin Delano Roosevelt, 1882–1945*

This is from President Roosevelt's message to Congress in January of 1941, when the battles of World War II were not going well for the Allies. It became known as the "Four Essential Freedoms" speech.

~

The wolf shall live with the lamb,
the leopard shall lie down with the kid,
the calf and the lion and the fatling together,
and a little child shall lead them.
The cow and the bear shall graze,
their young shall lie down together;
and the lion shall eat straw like the ox.
The nursing child shall play over the hole of the asp,
and the weaned child shall put its hand on the adder's den.

They will not hurt or destroy
on all my holy mountain;
for the earth will be full of the knowledge of the Lord
as the waters cover the sea.

—*Isaiah 11:6–9*

~

From childhood, I had read stories to comfort myself over the messiness of the world. Stories from the Old Testament had given me models of resourceful, independent children God approved of, like Joseph in Egypt, or Ruth. In college I was an English major. Now, recalling my childhood pleasure in Old Testament stories, I hit upon the idea of writing a graduate dissertation on the use of Old Testament imagery in the English metaphysical poets. In preparation for this work, I decided one morning to use the summer of 1963 before I began graduate work to learn some Hebrew at the seminary on campus. That afternoon I bought a copy of "Learning Hebrew by the Inductive Method" and a Hebrew Bible.

The next morning I had my coffee, took my books out of their bag, and laid them on my desk under the window. I studied chapter 1 of the grammar carefully. After that, I had another cup of coffee, and I laid the Hebrew Bible in front of me, opening it, as you do all Hebrew Bibles, back to front.

Then, as I stumbled through the first words of Genesis 1:1, "In the beginning, God created the heavens and the earth," I had an epiphany. Why this was so, I do not know, but I still recall the way the shape of the Hebrew letters and the look of the light falling on the creamy paper were mixed up with what I can only call a sense of cosmic goodness and joy in all created things I had never encountered before. It was as though the page itself were alive and the dots and tittles on the letters little flames. For the first time I could recall, life itself seemed all of a piece and trustworthy, and there was a place for me in it. In that instant I knew that God delighted in creation, in light, in water and mountains, in fruit-bearing trees and grasses, in water creatures and bugs, in wild animals and tame, in men and, most important for me, in women like me.

—*Roberta Bondi*

Bondi is professor of church history at the Candler School of Theology, Emory University, in Atlanta. This selection was taken from her book *Memories of God: Theological Reflections on a Life,* 1995.

~

Then I was standing on the highest mountain of them all, and round about beneath me was the whole hoop of the world. And while I stood there I saw more than I can tell and I understood more than I saw, for I was seeing in a sacred manner the shapes of all things in the spirit, and the shape of all shapes as they must live together like one being. And I saw that the sacred hoop of my people was one of many hoops that made one circle, wide as daylight and as starlight, and in the center grew one mighty flowering tree to shelter all the children of one mother and one father. And I saw it was holy.

—*Black Elk, 1862–1950*

The words and ideas of Black Elk, a Holy Man of the Oglala division of the Teton Sioux, were translated and recorded in a book entitled *Black Elk Speaks* (1988) by John Neihardt, from which this excerpt was taken.

~

What is to be done? How do we capture a new spirit and vision to meet the challenges of the post-industrial city, post-modern culture, and post-party politics?

First, we must admit that the most valuable sources for help, hope, and power consist of ourselves and our common history. As in the ages of Lincoln, Roosevelt, and King, we must look to new frameworks and languages to understand our multilayered crisis and overcome our deep malaise.

Second, we must focus our attention on the public square—the common good that undergirds our national and global destinies. The vitality of any public square ultimately depends on how much we care about the quality of our lives together. The neglect of our public infrastructure, for example—our water and sewage systems, bridges, tunnels, highways, subways, and streets—reflects not only our myopic economic policies, which impede productivity, but also the low priority we place on our common life.

The tragic plight of our children clearly reveals our deep disregard for public well-being. About one out of every five children in this country lives in poverty, including one out of every two black children and two out of every five Hispanic children. Most of our children—neglected by overburdened parents and bombarded by the market values of profit-hungry corporations—are ill-equipped to live lives of spiritual and cultural quality. Faced with these facts, how do we expect ever to constitute a vibrant society?

One essential step is some form of large-scale public intervention to ensure access to basic social goods—housing, food, health care, education, child care, and jobs. We must invigorate the common good with a mixture of government, business, and labor that does not follow any existing blueprint. After a period in which the private sphere has been sacralized and the public square gutted, the temptation is to make a fetish of the public square. We need to resist such dogmatic swings.

Last, the major challenge is to meet the need to generate new leadership. . . . Only a visionary leadership that can motivate "the better angels of our nature," as Lincoln said, and activate possibilities for a freer, more efficient, and stable America—only that leadership deserves cultivation and support.

—*Cornel West*

The author of *Race Matters,* from which this selection was taken, Cornel West is professor of religion and director of Afro-American Studies at Princeton University.

~

When I get to be a composer
I'm gonna write me some music about
Daybreak in Alabama.
And I'm gonna put the purtiest songs in it
Rising out of the ground like a swamp mist
And falling out of heaven like soft dew.
I'm gonna put some tall tall trees in it
And the scent of pine needles.
And the smell of red clay after rain

And long red necks
And poppy colored faces
And big brown arms
And the field daisy eyes
Of black and white black white black people
And I'm gonna put white hands
And black hands and brown and yellow hands
And red clay earth hands in it
Touching everybody with kind fingers
And touching each other natural as dew
In that dawn of music when I
Get to be a composer And write about daybreak
In Alabama.

—*Langston Hughes, 1902–1967*

One of America's foremost poets, Hughes was discovered by another famous poet, Vachel Lindsay, who read his poems to a fashionable audience in the very hotel in Washington, D.C., in which Hughes worked as a waiter.

~

The Interfaith Conference (of Metropolitan Washington) brings together the Islamic, Jewish, Protestant, Roman Catholic and Sikh faith communities in this region. . . .

Our commitment to act is drawn from the prophetic vision of a just and merciful world where each life is infinitely precious and where justice is the foundation for true peace. The Hebrew Bible and New Testament proclaim that every human being is formed in the image of God and envision a time when "justice will flow down like water and righteousness like an ever-flowing stream." The *Qur'an* emphasizes that every person is created in excellence, endowed with a nature that is good, and that all persons are to live justly with others. The Sikh scripture, the Guru Granth Sahib, identifies each one's soul with the supreme soul of God, and calls all Sikhs to defend the just cause of another. Such teachings undergird our common conviction that life is sacred and that the pursuit of peace with justice is a shared calling of all people of faith.

Today, as with our ancestors in faith, we are asked to choose life over death, good over evil, blessing over curse. Our prayers must go beyond calling for God's love to enter the hearts of others. Racism courses not only through bigots and haters. It flows through each one of us when we stand silent in the face of iniquity. Racism flows through each one of us when the color of another human being's skin colors our judgment about his or her humanity, character, intelligence, or competence. Thus our prayers must also call for God's love to enter more deeply into our own souls and psyches.

The current crisis in our nation is only a facet of a national problem of immense proportions. The violent responses expressed the anger and hopelessness shared by so many in our society. Racism, unemployment, lack of affordable housing and health care, poor education, drug abuse, and an increasing gap between rich and poor are compounded through unequal opportunity for economic progress and the disintegration of so many families. In many cases, political leadership has lacked the ability or moral courage to address these problems directly, saved only by the fact that the burden falls disproportionately on the socially and economically disadvantaged who have little power or influence.

But this crisis cannot be explained by social and economic conditions alone. For many there is also a sense of isolation and alienation, a profound lack of self-worth, a serious decline in moral behavior, a disturbing emphasis on one's own immediate gratification regardless of the community's welfare. There is a deep and abiding spiritual emptiness in the lives of so many people. Many young people especially feel no hope for their future.

There is no simple solution to the crisis we confront. We reaffirm our long-term commitment to treat the root causes of these problems in all segments of our community. They have festered for generations, and it will take many years to overcome the physical, psychological, and spiritual damage that has resulted. The problem is institutional, systemic, and pandemic. The task is monumental. The methods are varied and not yet all known, but the goal is clear:

All people must understand their human dignity, appreciate their self-worth, act on the realization that we are all brothers and sisters created by God, and develop a greater hope for the future based upon the concerted efforts of all segments of our community and country to build a just and peaceful society.

—*Interfaith Conference of Metropolitan Washington*

This excerpt is from the "Statement on the Challenges Facing Us in the Aftermath of the Verdict in the Rodney King Trial" that was endorsed by the Interfaith Conference in 1992. It also contained specific recommendations for community activities in support of its goal.

~

I believe in God, in the creative energy that "calls into existence the things that do not exist" (Romans 4:17), that is good and wants the good for us, which means being whole and flourishing in our ability to reflect God. The German word glauben (to believe) comes from the word geloben (to vow) and does not have as its first meaning the rational connotation of "to accept, to hold as true," but rather an existential dimension of "to promise oneself to someone." I believe in God for God's good creation, as it was intended, with equality of man and woman, with responsibility for tending and preserving the garden, with our ability to work and to love and thus to be the image of God.

The origin is at the same time the goal. Since we come from God, we also enter into God. Each day we take steps toward this reality of God. We recover partisanship for life from the triviality of the everyday and the trivialization of our life's goals and wishes. This recovery is what my tradition calls teshuva, or conversion, and one of the deepest experiences and hopes of the faith is the assumption—not guaranteed by anything secular—that we are capable of conversion. I should believe that of myself; disbelief in the possibility of one's own conversion is perhaps the worst thing that depression does to my friend. I am summoned and invited to think my neighbor capable of this conversion, even if he or she stubbornly continues on a course headed straight for an iceberg. . . . .

How, though, am I supposed to love God, praise and preserve creation, and take an active part in the kingdom without despairing? The help which my tradition offers to me is called Christ.

—*Dorothee Soelle*

This excerpt is from German theologian Soelle's *Theology for Skeptics: Reflections on God,* 1995.

~

Bill Moyers: At this moment we're sitting in the bosom of this great cathedral, St. John the Divine, where you often speak. Do the old traditions represented in this cathedral have anything to say about our modern problems of getting from here to the unknown?

Mary Bateson: This cathedral is a very special place, but it's special in a way that could be shared in many other places. The building is designed on a medieval pattern and represents ideas that go back two thousand and, indeed, four thousand years. At the same time, the artists that work here bring in the newest of the avant garde, and contemporary problems are discussed here. The cathedral's very much involved with AIDS, with homelessness, with the problems of the ghetto, which is, after all, just outside.

It is a mistake to shut out the new and just keep things as they are. But it is also a mistake to address the problems of the present and the future without reference to the traditions of the past. What the cathedral does Sunday after Sunday, and day after day, is to juxtapose new social problems and pains with ancient human efforts to understand and find solutions. That juxtaposition is the best stimulus both to responsibility in facing the unknown that lies ahead and to a certain serenity.

One of the things I talk about in the book I'm writing is that composing a life requires improvisation. It's like when, at six o'clock in the evening, four guests turn up, and your husband says, "We can feed them supper, can't we, darling?"

You go down to the kitchen, and you start scrambling through the refrigerator and the cupboards, trying to invent some combination that will make sense of the evening. Our past is full of wonderful traditions. The cupboards are full. The refrigerator is full. The situation calls for creative improvisation.

MOYERS: Do you think the day will come when you'll call home and say, "Dear, I'm bringing four guests home. Can you have dinner ready?" And *he* moves into action?

BATESON: I've done it.

MOYERS: He can improvise?

BATESON: We all can improvise—and we're all going to have to.

—*Mary Catherine Bateson and Bill Moyers*

This dialogue took place as part of a public television program that also became a book entitled *Bill Moyers: A World of Ideas—Conversations with Thoughtful Men and Women about American Life Today and the Ideas Shaping Our Future* (1989). Bateson is professor of anthropology at George Mason University.

~

What do we mean when we say that first of all we seek liberty? I often wonder whether we do not rest our hopes too much upon constitutions, upon laws and upon courts. These are false hopes; believe me, these are false hopes. Liberty lies in the hearts of men and women; when it dies there, no constitution, no law, no court can save it; no constitution, no law, no court can even do much to help it. While it lies there it needs no constitution, no law, no court to save it. And what is this liberty which must lie in the hearts of men and women? It is not the ruthless, the unbridled will; it is not freedom to do as one likes. That is the denial of liberty and leads straight to its overthrow. A society in which we recognize no check upon our freedom soon becomes a society where freedom is the possession of only a savage few, as we have learned to our sorrow.

What then is the spirit of liberty? I cannot define it; I can only tell you my own faith. The spirit of liberty is the spirit which is not too sure that it is right; the spirit of liberty is the spirit which seeks to understand the minds of other men and women; the spirit of liberty is the spirit which weighs their interests alongside its own without bias; the spirit of liberty remembers that not even a sparrow falls to earth unheeded; the spirit of liberty is the spirit of One who, near two thousand years ago, taught [humankind] that lesson it has never learned, but has never quite forgotten: that there may be a realm where the least shall be heard and considered side by side with the greatest.

—*Judge Learned Hand, 1872–1961;* alt.

Judge Hand spoke these words in an address made at the "I Am an American Day" ceremony in Central Park, New York City, May 21, 1944.

~

Half of each year I live and work in Prague, but for forty-two years I have lived and worked in America. I am struck much more by the similarities than by any difference. The social disintegration in the lands of the former Soviet empire seems to me simply to bring out in stark relief what in the West has been masked by affluence but is no less present—the weakness of a civilization that has lost its legitimating vision, its sense of reality and of personal responsibility. For some three hundred years, that civilization lived in the illusion that the pursuit of happiness could be supplanted by the pursuit of property. The Soviet empire discredited the idea by failing in the latter pursuit, the West by succeeding far too well, but the moral is the same: the pursuit of property is not a substitute for a legitimating vision.

I am convinced that if our civilization is to survive—and if the former "East" is to halt its progressive disintegration—we all need to learn that happiness is not to be found in acquiring but in giving, not in exploitation but in caring, not in self-gratification but in self-transcendence.

—*Erazim Kohák*

This excerpt came from an article entitled "Ashes, Ashes . . . Central Europe after Forty Years" by Kohák in the spring 1992 issue of *Daedalus.* Kohák is professor of philosophy at Boston University and at Charles University in Prague.

~

May there be welfare to all beings;
  may there be fullness and wholeness to all people;
  may there be constant good and auspicious life to
    everyone;
  may there be peace everywhere. . . .
May all be full of happiness and abundance;
  may everyone in the world enjoy complete health,
    free from diseases;
  may all see and experience good things in their lives,

may not even a single person experience sorrow and misery.
OM. Peace! Peace! Peace!

—*A Hindu Daily Prayer*

Hinduism is the oldest and considered the most complex of the contemporary world religions. Believers primarily are in or from India.

~

We Declare:

We are interdependent. Each of us depends on the well-being of the whole, and so we have respect for the community of living beings, for people, animals, and plants, and for the preservation of Earth, the air, water, and soil.

We take individual responsibility for all we do. All our decisions, actions, and failures to act have consequences.

We must treat others as we wish others to treat us. We make a commitment to respect life and dignity, individuality and diversity, so that every person is treated humanely, without exception. We must have patience and acceptance. We must be able to forgive, learning from the past but never allowing ourselves to be enslaved by memories of hate. Opening our hearts to one another, we must sink our narrow differences for the cause of the world community, practicing a culture of solidarity and relatedness.

We consider humankind our family. We must strive to be kind and generous. We must not live for ourselves alone, but should also serve others, never forgetting the children, the aged, the poor, the suffering, the disabled, the refugees, and the lonely. No person should ever be considered or treated as a second-class citizen, or be exploited in any way whatsoever. There should be equal partnership between men and women. We must not commit any kind of sexual immorality. We must put behind us all forms of domination or abuse.

We commit ourselves to a culture of nonviolence, respect, justice, and peace. We shall not oppress, injure, torture, or kill other human beings, forsaking violence as a means of settling differences.

We must strive for a just social and economic order, in which everyone has an equal chance to reach full potential as a human being. We must speak and act truthfully and with compassion, dealing fairly with all, and avoiding prejudice and hatred. We must not steal. We must move beyond the dominance of greed for power, prestige, money, and consumption to make a just and peaceful world.

Earth cannot be changed for the better unless the consciousness of individuals is changed first. We pledge to increase our awareness by disciplining our minds, by meditation, by prayer, or by positive thinking. Without risk and a readiness to sacrifice there can be no fundamental change in our situation. Therefore we commit ourselves to this global ethic, to understanding one another, and to socially beneficial, peace-fostering, and nature-friendly ways of life.

We invite all people, whether religious or not, to do the same.

—*Parliament of the World's Religions, 1993*

The first Parliament of the World's Religions was held at the 1893 World's Columbian Exposition in Chicago. The second, held in Chicago one hundred years later, issued a document "Towards a Global Ethic" from which this was taken.

~

Our hope is that the world's religious leaders and the rulers thereof will unitedly arise for the reformation of this age and the rehabilitation of its fortunes. Let them, after meditating on its needs, take counsel together and through anxious and full deliberation, administer to a diseased and sorely afflicted world the remedy it requires.

—*Bahá'u'lláh, 1817–1892*

Bahá'u'lláh is the Persian founder of the Bahá'í faith and writer of more than one hundred volumes of scripture, most while he was in prison for his beliefs.

~

The goal of a politics of meaning is to change the bottom line in American society, so that productivity or efficiency of corporations, legislation, or social practices is no longer measured solely by the degree to which they maximize wealth and power—but rather also by the degree to which they tend to maximize our capacities to sustain loving and caring relationships and to be ethically, spiritually, and ecologically sensitive.

—*Michael Lerner*

Editor of *Tikkun* magazine, Lerner leads workshops and seminars around the country on "the politics of meaning," also the title of his book.

~

I am in favor of a political system based on the citizen, and recognizing all . . . fundamental civil and human rights in their universal validity, and equally applied: that is, no member of a single race, a single nation, a single sex, or a single religion may be endowed with basic rights that are any different from anyone else's. In other words, I am in favor of what is called a civic society.

Today this civic principle is sometimes presented as if it stood in opposition to the principle of national affiliation, creating the impression that it ignores or suppresses the aspect of our home represented by our nationality. This is a crude misunderstanding of that principle. On the contrary, I support the civic principle because it represents the best way for individuals to realize themselves, to fulfill their identity in all the circles of their home, to enjoy everything that belongs to their natural world, not just some aspects of it. To establish a state on any other principle than the civic principle—on the principle of ideology, of nationality or religion, for instance—means making one aspect of our home superior to all the others, and thus reduces us as people, reduces our natural world. And that hardly ever leads to anything good. Most wars and revolutions, for example, came about precisely because of this one-dimensional conception of the state.

—*Vaclav Havel*

Havel is the president of the Czech Republic, a playwright, and the author of many books, including *The Art of the Impossible: Politics as Morality in Practice* (1997), translated by Paul Wilson. This excerpt is from a 1991 speech.

~

The American identity will never be fixed and final; it will always be in the making. Changes in the population have always brought changes in the national ethics and will continue to do so; but not, one must hope, at the expense of national integration. The question America confronts as a pluralistic society is how to vindicate cherished cultures and traditions without breaking the bonds of cohesion—common ideals, common political institutions, common language, common culture, common fate—that hold the republic together.

Our task is to combine due appreciation of the splendid diversity of the nation with due emphasis on the great unifying Western ideas of individual freedom, political democracy, and human rights. These are the ideas that define the American nationality—and that today empower people of all continents, races, and creeds.

—*Arthur M. Schlesinger Jr.*

Political commentator Schlesinger is the author of numerous books on the presidency and the nation. This excerpt was taken from his book *The Disuniting of America,* 1992.

~

Society's powerful, materialistic vision of progress seems to leave little room for the gentler, more loving vision which also finds a home in us. This is the vision of the heart and spirit we all share: the vision in which progress means caring for creation, for each other, for the earth and the environment we live in; building a peaceful community and world; and living harmoniously together, with fairness and justice. With such a vision we are moved by love.

—*Daniel Gómez-Ibáñez*

Dr. Gómez-Ibáñez is executive director of the International Committee for the Peace Council, Cambridge, Wisconsin, and a trustee of the Council for a Parliament of the World's Religions.

~

JOHN THE EVANGELIST: Master, what is holiness? Is it just to keep the Commandments and say the right prayers, and do the right things, and pay the proper dues, as the priests tell us? Or is it something quite different? The preaching of John the Baptist has troubled our hearts, and the great prophets have terrified us with their thunderings against sin. We are disheartened, because nothing we do seems to be any good, and the righteous God is so great and terrible and far away. How can we rise so far above ourselves? What sort of heroic thing is holiness?

JESUS: The priests are right, and the prophets are right too. I haven't come to take away the Law, but to show you how to keep it. This is holiness—to love, and be ruled by love; for love can do no wrong.

JOHN THE EVANGELIST: As simple as all that?

JESUS: So simple that a child can understand it. So simple that only children really can understand it.

ANDREW: But what has all this to do with the coming of the Kingdom?

JESUS: It is the Kingdom. Wherever there is love, there is the Kingdom of God.

—*Dorothy Sayers, 1893–1957*

During the early days of World War II, author Dorothy Sayers wrote a radio play, "The King's Herald," on the life of Christ for the British Broadcasting Corporation. The plays appeared in a book entitled *The Man Born to Be King: A Play-Cycle on the Life of Our Lord and Saviour Jesus Christ* in 1943, from which this excerpt was taken.

~

Therefore, let us work, let us develop all our possibilities; not for ourselves, but for our fellow-creatures. Let us be enlightened in our efforts, let us strive after the general welfare of humanity and indeed of all creation. We are born here to do certain things. Life may be misery or not; it concerns us not; let us do what we have to do. We are not here wholly alone . . . we cannot save ourselves unless others are saved. We cannot advance unless the general progress is assured. We must help one another, we must abandon our vulgar egocentric ideas, we must expand ourselves so that the whole universe is identified with us, and so that our interests are those of humanity. The attainment of Nirvana and the manifestation of the Buddhist life are possible only through the denial of selfhood and through the united labor of all our fellow creatures.

—*Soyen Shaku, 1859–1919*

Soyen Shaku is a Buddhist monk and Zen master whose writings have been translated and published in *Zen for Americans* (1974), from which this excerpt was taken. The translator is D. T. Suzuki.

~

I see the vision of a poor weak soul striving after good. It was not cut short; and in the end it learned, through tears and much pain, that holiness is an infinite compassion for others; that greatness is to take the common things of life, and walk truly among them. That . . . happiness is a great love and much serving.

—*Olive Schreiner, 1855–1920*

Growing up on a farm in South Africa, Olive Schreiner became a writer about her homeland. Howard Thurman collected some of her work in *A Track to the Water's Edge: An Olive Schreiner Reader,* 1973, from which this excerpt was taken.

~

Then I saw a new heaven and a new earth; for the first heaven and the first earth had passed away and the sea was no more. And I saw the holy city, the new Jerusalem, coming down out of heaven from God, prepared as a bride and bridegroom adorned for each other; and I heard a loud voice from the throne saying:

"See, the home of God is among mortals.
God will dwell with them,
they shall be God's people,
and God indeed will be with them,
God will wipe every tear from their eyes,
Death will be no more;
mourning and crying and pain will be no more,
for the first things have passed away."
And the one who sat upon the throne said, "See, I am making all things new."

—*Revelation 21:1–5a*

II

"Forgive Us Our Trespasses"

The Need for Mercy

Every gun that is made, every warship launched,
every rocket fired signifies a theft from those who hunger and
are not fed, those who are cold and not clothed.

This world in arms is not spending money alone.
It is spending the sweat of its laborers, the genius of its scientists,
the hope of its children.

—President Dwight David Eisenhower, 1890–1969

While we know we could do better to move our society toward the goals and visions of the common good, we can become paralyzed by the enormity of the tasks before us. What can we do to prevent social tragedies like drug abuse or global horrors like wars? A sense of inadequacy that can lead to despair can be turned into a sense of humility that can lead to hope if we confess our own participation in a materialistic and self-centered society before almighty God and ask forgiveness. Scripture assures us of God's mercy and of continuing possibilities for renewal. We are not powerless. We do have resources. We can do better as individuals and as a nation. The readings that follow remind us of these spiritual realities.

Create in me a clean heart, O God,
and renew a right spirit with me.
Cast me not away from thy presence;
and take not thy holy spirit from me.
Restore unto me the joy of thy salvation;
and uphold me with thy free spirit.

—*Psalm 51:10–12*

The concern which I lay bare before God today is:
My concern for the life of the world in these
troubled times.
I confess my own inner confusion as I look out
upon the world.
There is food for all—many are hungry.
There are clothes enough for all—many are in rags.
There is room enough for all—many are crowded.
There are none who want war—preparations for
conflict abound.
I confess my own share in the ills of the times.
I have shirked my own responsibilities as a citizen.
I have not been wise in casting my ballot.
I have left to others a real interest in making
a public opinion
worthy of democracy.
I have been concerned about my own little job, my
own little security,
my own shelter, my own bread.
I have not really cared about jobs for others,
security for others,
shelter for others, bread for others.

I have not worked for peace; I want peace,
    but I have voted and worked for war.
I have silenced my own voice that it may not be heard
    on the side of any cause, however right,
        if it meant running
    risks or damaging my own little reputation.
Let Thy light burn in me that I may, from this moment on, take effective steps within my own powers, to live up to the light and courageously to pay for the kind of world I so deeply desire.

—*Howard Thurman, 1900–1981*

A prolific writer, Thurman also was a professor of religion at several colleges and a Baptist preacher described as a premier African American spiritual leader. This prayer comes from his book *Meditations of the Heart.*

~

At the beginning of each meal, I recommend that you look at your plate and silently recite, "My plate is empty now, but I know that it is going to be filled with delicious food in just a moment." While waiting to be served or to serve yourself, I suggest you breathe three times and look at it even more deeply, [saying,] "At this very moment many, many people around the world are also holding a plate, but their plate is going to be empty for a long time."

Forty thousand children die each day because of the lack of food. Children alone. We can be very happy to have such wonderful food, but we also suffer because we are capable of seeing. But when we see in this way, it makes us sane, because the way in front of us is clear—the way to live so that we can make peace with ourselves and with the world.

When we see the good and the bad, the wondrous and the deep suffering, we have to live in a way that we can make peace between ourselves and the world.

—*Thích Nhât Hanh;* alt.

A Buddhist monk from Vietnam and leader in the Buddhist Peace Fellowship, Thích Nhât Hanh is a popular writer of prayers and meditations used in ecumenical services. This excerpt is from his book *The Heart of Understanding.*

~

O God, forgive our rich nation where small babies
die of cold quite legally.
O God, forgive our rich nation where small children suffer
from hunger quite legally.
O God, forgive our rich nation where toddlers and
school children die from guns sold quite legally.
O God, forgive our rich nation that lets children
be the poorest group of citizens quite legally.
O God, forgive our rich nation that lets the rich
continue to get more at the expense of the poor
quite legally.
O God, forgive our rich nation which thinks security
rests in missiles rather than in mothers, and in bombs
rather than in babies.
O God, forgive our rich nation for not giving you
sufficient thanks by giving to others their daily bread.
O God, help us never to confuse what is quite legal
with what is just and right in Your sight.

—*Marian Wright Edelman*

Eloquent leader of the Washington march to Stand for Children, Edelman is the head of the Children's Defense Fund and author of *Guide My Feet: Prayers and Meditations for Our Children,* from which this prayer was taken.

~

If only there were evil people somewhere insidiously committing evil deeds and it were necessary only to separate them from the rest of us and destroy them. But the line dividing good and evil cuts through the heart of every human being. And who is willing to destroy a piece of his own heart?

—*Aleksandr I. Solzhenitsyn*

Writing of the evils of a Russian prison system following the revolution, Solzhenitsyn's works earned him the Nobel Prize for literature in 1970 and a long exile in America. This excerpt is taken from *The Gulag Archipelago.*

~

[Father Brown said] "I don't try to get outside the man. I try to get inside the murderer. . . . Indeed it' s much more than that, don' t you see? I am inside a man. I am always inside a man, moving his arms and legs; but I wait till I know I am inside a murderer, thinking his thoughts, wrestling with his passions; till I have bent myself into the posture of his hunched and peering hatred; till I see the world with his bloodshot and squinting eyes, looking between the blinkers of his half-witted concentration; looking up the short and sharp perspective of a straight road to a pool of blood. Till I am really a murderer."

"Oh," said Mr. Chace, regarding him with a long grim face, and added: "And that is what you call a religious exercise."

"Yes," said Father Brown. "That is what I call a religious exercise."

After an instant's silence he resumed, "It's so real a religious exercise that I'd rather not have said anything about it. But I simply couldn't have you going off and telling all your countrymen that I had a secret magic connected with Thought-Forms, could I? I've put it badly, but it' s true. No man's really any good till he knows how bad he is, or might be; till he's realised exactly how much right he has to all this snobbery, and sneering, and talking about 'criminals,' as if they were apes in a forest ten thousand miles away; till he's got rid of all the dirty self-deception of talking about low types and deficient skulls; till he's squeezed out of his soul the last drop of the oil of the Pharisees; till his only hope is somehow or other to have captured one criminal, and kept him safe and sane under his own hat."

—*G. K. Chesterton, 1874–1936*

British author and critic Gilbert Keith Chesterton was an active Roman Catholic. The hero of his series of detective stories is a priest. This excerpt is taken from *The Secret of Father Brown.*

~

Our God and God of our [forebears], let our prayer reach You—do not turn away from our pleading. For we are not so arrogant and obstinate [as] to claim that we are indeed righteous people and have never sinned. But we know that both we and our [forebears] have sinned.

We have abused and betrayed. We are cruel.
We have destroyed and embittered other people's lives.
We were false to ourselves.
We have gossiped about others and hated them.
We have insulted and jeered. We have killed.
 We have lied.
We have misled others and neglected them.
We were obstinate. We have perverted and quarrelled.
We have robbed and stolen.
We have transgressed through unkindness.
We have been both violent and weak.
We have practised extortion.
We have yielded to wrong desires, our zeal
 was misplaced.

We turn away from Your commandments and good judgement but it does not help us. Your justice exists whatever happens to us, for You work for truth, but we bring about evil. What can we say before You—so distant is the place where You are found? And what can we tell You—Your being is remote as the heavens? Yet You know everything, hidden and revealed. You know the mysteries of the universe and the intimate secrets of everyone alive. You probe our body's state. You see into the heart and mind. Nothing escapes You, nothing is hidden from Your gaze. Our God and God of our [forebears], have mercy on us and pardon all our sins; grant atonement for all our iniquities, forgiveness for all our transgressions.

—*Day of Atonement;* alt.

The beginning of the religious year for Jews is a solemn observance of the Day of Atonement, Yom Kippur, a period of spiritual introspection. This prayer is from *Forms of Prayer for Jewish Worship,* 1977.

~

There's a wideness in God's mercy, like the wideness
of the sea;
There's a kindness in God's justice which is more
than liberty.
There's no place where earthly sorrows are more felt
than in God's heaven;
There's no place where earthly failings have such kindly
judgment given.

For the love of God is broader than the measures
of our minds;
And the heart of the Eternal is most wonderfully kind.
If our love were but more faithful, we would gladly trust
God's word;
And our lives would show thanksgiving for the goodness
of our God.

—*Frederick William Faber, 1814–1863;* alt.

A French Roman Catholic priest, Frederick William Faber wrote 150 hymns to correspond to the number of psalms.

~

And whereas, it is the duty of nations as well as of [citizens] to own their dependence upon the overruling power of God, to confess their sins and transgressions in humble sorrow yet with assured hope that genuine repentance will lead to mercy and pardon, and to recognize the sublime truth, announced in the Holy Scriptures and proven by all history: that those nations only are blessed whose God is the Lord:

And, insomuch as we know that, by [God's] divine law, nations like individuals are subjected to punishments and chastisement in this world, may we not justly fear that the awful calamity of civil war, which now desolates the land may be a punishment inflicted upon us for our presumptuous sins to the needful end of our national reformation as a whole people?

We have been the recipients of the choicest bounties of Heaven. We have been preserved these many years in peace and prosperity. We have grown in numbers, wealth and power as no other nation has ever grown.

But we have forgotten God. We have forgotten the gracious Hand which preserved us in peace, and multiplied and enriched and strengthened us; and we have vainly imagined, in the deceitfulness of our hearts, that all these blessings were produced by some superior wisdom and virtue of our own.

Intoxicated with unbroken success, we have become too self-sufficient to feel the necessity of redeeming and preserving grace, too proud to pray to the God that made us!

It behooves us then to humble ourselves before the offended Power, to confess our national sins and to pray for clemency and forgiveness.

—*Abraham Lincoln, 1809–1865;* alt.

This excerpt from a "Proclamation Appointing a National Fast Day" was distributed by President Lincoln on March 30, 1863, in the midst of some of the worst days of the Civil War.

~

Tao adjusts excess and deficiency so that there is perfect balance. It takes from what is too much and gives to what isn't enough. Those who try to control, who use force to protect their power, go against the direction of the Tao. They take from those who don't have enough and give to those who have far too much.

—*Lao-tzu, 6th century* B.C.E.

Lao Tzu (the Old Master) was a contemporary of Confucius and a keeper of the Chinese imperial library. He prepared the *Tao Te Ching (Book of Tao and Virtue),* which became the guide for followers. This excerpt is from that book.

~

Now we're going to march again, and we've got to march again, in order to put the issue where it is supposed to be. And force everybody to see that there are thirteen hundred of God's children here suffering, sometimes going hungry, going through dark and dreary nights wondering how this thing is going to come out. That's the issue. And we've got to say to the nation: we know how it's coming out. For when people get caught up with that which is right and they are willing to sacrifice for it, there is no stopping point short of victory.

It's alright to talk about "long white robes over yonder," in all of its symbolism. But ultimately people want some suits and dresses and shoes to wear down here. It's alright to talk about "streets flowing with milk and honey," but God has commanded us to be concerned about the slums down here, and his children who can't eat three square meals a day. It's alright to talk about the new Jerusalem, but one day, God's preacher must talk about the New York, the new Atlanta, the new Philadelphia, the new Los Angeles, the new Memphis, Tennessee. This is what we have to do.

—*Martin Luther King Jr., 1929–1968*

This excerpt is from a speech now entitled "I've Been to the Mountaintop" delivered by King before a protest march in Memphis, Tennessee, in 1963.

~

Here, then, are some of the bitter fruits of that inveterate prejudice which the vast proportion of northern women are cherishing towards their colored sisters; and let us remember that every one of us who denies the sinfulness of this prejudice . . . is awfully guilty in the sight of Him who is no respecter of persons. . . .

But our colored sisters are oppressed in other ways. As they walk the streets of our cities, they are continually liable to be insulted with the vulgar epithet of "nigger"; no matter how respectable or wealthy, they cannot visit the Zoological Institute of New York except in the capacity of nurses or servants—no matter how worthy, they cannot gain admittance into or receive assistance from any of the charities of this City. In Philadelphia, they are cast out of our widow's Asylum, and their children are refused admittance to the House of Refuge, the Orphan's House and the Infant School connected with the Alms-House, though into these are gathered the very offscouring of our population.

These are only specimens of that soul-crushing influence from which the colored women of the north are daily suffering. Then, again, some of them have been robbed of their husbands and children by the heartless kidnapper [slaveowners], and others have themselves been dragged into slavery. If they attempt to travel, they are exposed to great indignities and great inconveniences. Instances have been known of their actually dying in consequence of the exposure to which they were subjected on board of our steamboats. No money could purchase the use of a berth for a delicate female because she had a colored skin.

Prejudice, then, degrades and fetters the minds, persecutes and murders the bodies of our free colored sisters. Shall we be silent at such a time of this?

—*Angelina Grimké, 1805–1879*

Angelina and Sarah Grimké grew up in South Carolina in a slaveholding family. Both sisters rebelled and became Quakers, abolitionists, and feminists. This speech in 1838 was called "An Appeal to the Women of the Nominally Free States."

~

Our [God], bring to the remembrance of Thy people Thine ancient and time-honored promise: "If my people, which are called by my name, shall humble themselves, and pray, and seek my face, and turn from their wicked ways, then will I hear from heaven, and will forgive their sin, and will heal their land."

We—this company of Thy people assembled—would begin now to meet the conditions that will enable Thee to fulfill Thy promise.

May all of America come to understand that right-living alone exalteth a nation, that only in Thy will can peace and joy be found. But, [God], this land cannot be righteous unless her people are righteous, and we, here gathered, are part of America. We know that the world cannot be changed until [our] hearts are changed. Our hearts need to be changed.

We therefore confess to Thee that:
Wrong ideas and sinful living have cut us off
from Thee.
We have been greedy.
We have sought to hide behind barricades of selfishness;
shackles have imprisoned the great heart of America.
We have tried to isolate ourselves from the bleeding
wounds of a blundering world.
In our self-sufficiency we have sought not Thy help.
We have held conferences and ignored Thee
completely.
We have disguised selfishness as patriotism;
our arrogance has masqueraded as pride.
We have frittered away time and opportunities while the
world bled.
Our ambitions have blinded us to opportunities.
We have bickered in factory and business, and
sought to solve our differences only through
self-interest.

[O] God of Hosts, forgive us! O God, by Thy guidance and Thy power may our beloved land once again become God's own country, a nation contrite in heart, confessing her sins; a nation sensitive to all the unresolved injustice and wrong still in our midst.

Hear this our prayer and grant that we may confidently expect to see it answered in our time, through Jesus Christ. . . . Amen.

—*Peter Marshall, 1902–1949;* alt.

Peter Marshall was pastor of New York Avenue Presbyterian Church in Washington, D.C., when he became chaplain to the U.S. Senate in 1948. This selection is from *The Prayers of Peter Marshall,* 1954.

~

Lack of virtue is a very harmful quality in us.
Bad habits harm us in every way.
Earthly desire kills in us the word of God.
Wilful obstinacy wreaks much havoc in us.
Enmity of heart drives out the Holy Spirit.
An angry heart robs us of God's intimacy.
False piety can never endure,
But the true love of God shall never pass.
And if we do not flee these enemies,
Then they shall steal Paradise from us.
For we make a heaven on earth
When we lead a holy life here below.

—*Mechthild of Magdeburg, 1212–1282*

German mystic Mechthild of Magdeburg was a member of the Beguines of medieval Europe, laywomen who lived apart in pious communities practicing chastity, simplicity, poverty, manual labor, and service to the poor. This excerpt is from *The Flowing Light of the Godhead,* the work for which she is best known.

~

Two men went up to the temple to pray, one a Pharisee and the other a tax collector. The Pharisee, standing by himself, was praying thus, "God, I thank you that I am not like other people: thieves, rogues, adulterers, or even like this tax collector. I fast twice a week; I give a tenth of all my income."

But the tax collector, standing far off, would not even look up to heaven, but was beating his breast and saying, "God, be merciful to me, a sinner!"

I tell you, this man went down to his home justified rather than the other; for all who exalt themselves will be humbled, but all who humble themselves will be exalted.

—*Luke 18:10–14*

~

O, the agony of the embattled spirit in the anguished
grapple with pride!
Pride of achievement, pride of bitterness—
Pride of the broken heart, pride of silent suffering
Pride of love and hatred
Pride of husband and wife
Pride of parent and child
Pride of class and race
Pride of nation and flag
Pride of righteousness and lust—

O, the agony of the embattled spirit in the anguished
grapple with pride!
Teach us, our Father, the precious clue to honesty!
Grant that where we are, in what we do
Life need take no offense in us!
Search us, knead us, remove from us
The spots, the blemishes, even the shadows
That sent us forth in our own light
Shielded from Thy radiance and Thy fullness.

—*Howard Thurman, 1899–1981*

Thurman, a Baptist minister and teacher, was deeply influenced by the Quakers. He taught religion at Morehouse and Spelman Colleges and was dean at Rankin Chapel at Howard University until 1944.

~

I have always maintained that violence is evil. But I also think it is clear that there are some practices of violence that are worse than others. Every act of violence is evil, but on some occasions it may very well be that violence is inevitable. In that sense, liberation theology has insisted that the gravest form of violence, and the root of every other kind of violence, is structural violence, that is, the violence of a civilization of capital which keeps the vast majority of humanity in biological, cultural, social, and political conditions that are absolutely inhuman.

The civilization of capital is the most basic form of structural violence. Therefore, to say that liberation theologians defend violence or that they promote violence is wrong. In reality, liberation theology is that theology which has most systematically denounced structural violence. Of course, nobody accuses the structural order of being "violent" since it just seems to be the normal state of affairs, a reflection of the established order, etc.

—*Ignacio Ellacuría, d. 1989*

Theologian, author, and former rector of the University of Central America in El Salvador, Ellacuria was assassinated along with five of his Jesuit brothers and two Salvadoran women in October 1989. This reading is from *New Visions for the Americas,* 1993.

~

God All-Seeing:
I ought to have thought, but I have not thought;
I ought to have spoken, but I have not spoken;
I ought to have acted, but I have not acted—as it was the will of thy Good Spirit,
I repent for that sin with thought, word, and deed.

I ought not to have thought, but I have thought;
I ought not to have spoken, but I have spoken;
I ought not to have acted, but I have acted, as it was the will of the Evil Spirit,
I repent of that sin with my thought, word, and deed.

—*A Zoroastrian Prayer, ca. 8th century* B.C.E.

The founder of Zoroastrianism, Zoroaster was a Persian prophet who taught a monotheistic view of God, whom he called Ahura Mazda. This selection was translated by Jivanji Jamshadji Modi.

~

Because there is global insecurity, nations are engaged in a mad arms race, spending billions of dollars wastefully on instruments of destruction, when millions are starving. And yet, just a fraction of what is expended so obscenely on defense budgets would make the difference in enabling God's children to fill their stomachs, be educated, and be given the chance to lead fulfilled and happy lives. We have the capacity to feed ourselves several times over, but we are daily haunted by the spectacle of the gaunt dregs of humanity shuffling along in endless queues, with bowls to collect what the charity of the world has provided, too little, too late.

When will we learn, when will the people of the world get up and say, Enough is enough. God created us for fellowship. God created us so that we should form the human family, existing together because we were made for one another. We are not made for an exclusive self-sufficiency but for interdependence, and we break the law of our being at our peril.

—*Desmond Mpilo Tutu*

Archbishop Tutu, chair of the Commission on Truth and Reconciliation in South Africa, seeks to reconcile a nation torn by the evils of apartheid. This reading is from his Nobel Peace Prize address in 1984.

~

The leaders of the movement trembled on seeing a tall, gaunt black woman in a gray dress and white turban, surmounted with an uncouth sun-bonnet, march deliberately into the church, walk with the air of a queen up the aisle, and take her seat upon the pulpit steps. A buzz of disapprobation was heard all over the house, and there fell on the listening ear, "An abolition affair!" "Women's rights and niggers!" "I told you so!" "Go it, darkey!"

. . . Morning, afternoon, and evening exercises came and went. Through all these sessions old Sojourner, quiet and reticent as the "Lybian Statue," sat crouched against the wall on the corner of the pulpit stairs, her sun-bonnet shading her eyes, her elbows on her knees, her chin resting upon her broad, hard palms. At intermission she was busy selling The Life of Sojourner Truth, a narrative of her own strange and adventurous life. Again and again, timorous and trembling ones came to me and said, with earnestness, "Don't let her speak, Mrs. Gage, it will ruin us. Every newspaper in the land will have our cause mixed up with abolition and niggers, and we shall be utterly denounced." My only answer was, "We shall see when the time comes."

The second day the work waxed warm. Methodist, Baptist, Episcopal, Presbyterian, and Universalist ministers came in to hear and discuss the resolutions presented. One claimed superior rights and privileges of man, on the ground of "superior intellect"; another because of the "manhood of Christ; if God had desired the equality of woman, He would have given some token of his will through the birth, life, and death of the Saviour." Another gave us a theological view of the "sin of the first mother."

There were very few women in those days who dared to "speak in meeting"; and the august teachers of the people were seemingly getting the better of us, while the boys in the galleries, and the sneerers among the pews, were hugely enjoying the discomfiture, as they supposed, of the "strong-minded." Some of the tender-skinned friends were on the point of losing dignity, and the atmosphere betokened a storm. Then, slowly from her seat in the corner rose Sojourner Truth, who, till now, had scarcely lifted her head. "Don't let her speak!" gasped half a dozen in my ear. She moved slowly and solemnly to the front, laid her old bonnet at her feet, and turned her great speaking eyes to me. There was a hissing sound of disapprobation above and below. I rose and announced, "Sojourner Truth," and begged the audience to keep silence for a few moments.

The tumult subsided at once, and every eye was fixed on this almost Amazon form, which stood nearly six feet high, head erect, and eyes piercing the upper air like one in a dream. At her first word there was a profound hush. She spoke in deep tones, which, though not loud, reached every ear in the house, and away through the throng at the doors and windows.

"Wall, children, whar dar is so much racket dar must be somethin' out o' kilter. I think dat 'twixt de niggers of de Souf and de womin at de Norf, all talkin' 'bout rights, de white men will be in a fix pretty soon. But what's all dis here talkin' 'bout?

"Dat man ober dar say dat womin needs to be helped into carriages, and lifted over ditches, and to hab de best place everywhar. Nobody eber helps me into carriages, or ober mud puddles, or gibs me any best place!" And raising herself to her full height, and her voice to a pitch like rolling thunder, she asked, "And a'n't I a woman? Look at me! Look at my arm!" (And she bared her right arm to the shoulder, showing her tremendous muscular power.) "I have ploughed, and planted, and gathered into barns, and no man could head me! And a'n't I a womin? I could work as much and eat as much as a man—when I could get it—and bear de lash as well! And a'n't I a woman? I have borne thirteen children, and see 'em mos' all sold off to slavery, and when I cried out with my mother's grief, none but Jesus heard me! And a'n't I a woman?

"Den dey talks 'bout dis ting in de head; what dis dey call it?" ("Intellect," whispered someone near.) "Dat's it, honey. What's dat got to do wid womin's rights or niggers' rights? If my cup won't hold but a pint, and yourn holds a quart, wouldn't ye be mean not to let me have my little half-measure full?" And she pointed her significant finger, and sent a keen glance at the minister who had made the argument. The cheering was long and loud.

"Den dat little man in black dar, he say women can't have

as much rights as men, 'cause Christ wan't a woman! Whar did your Christ come from?" Rolling thunder couldn't have stilled that crowd, as did those deep, wonderful tones, as she stood there with outstretched arms and eyes of fire. Raising her voice still louder, she repeated, "Whar did your Christ come from? From God and a woman! Man had nothin' to do wid Him." Oh, what a rebuke that was to that little man!

Turning again to another objector, she took up the defense of Mother Eve. I cannot follow her through it all. It was pointed, and witty, and solemn; eliciting at almost every sentence deafening applause; and she ended by asserting: "If de fust woman God ever made was strong enough to turn de world upside down all alone, dese women togedder (and she glanced her eye over the platform) ought to be able to turn it back, and get it right side up again! And now dey is asking to do it, de men better let 'em." Long-continued cheering greeted this. "Bleeged to ye for hearin' on me, and now old Sojourner han't got nothin' more to say."

Amid roars of applause, she returned to her corner, leaving more than one of us with streaming eyes and hearts beating with gratitude. She had taken us up in her strong arms and carried us safely over the slough of difficulty, turning the whole tide in our favor. I have never in my life seen anything like the magical influence that subdued the mobbish spirit of the day, and turned the sneers and jeers of an excited crowd into the notes of respect and admiration. Hundreds rushed up to shake hands with her, and congratulate the glorious old mother, and bid her God-speed on her mission of "testifyin' agin concerning the wickedness of this 'ere people."

—*Article about Sojourner Truth, 1797–1883*

Frances D. Gage wrote "Sojourner Truth 'Speaks in Meeting' " after a women's rights event in Akron, Ohio, in 1851. It first appeared in the book *History of Woman's Suffrage* in 1881.

~

Perhaps it is no wonder that the women were first at the Cradle and last at the Cross. They had never known a man like this Man—there never has been such another. A prophet and teacher who never nagged at them, never flattered or coaxed or patronised; who never made arch jokes about them, never treated them either as "The women, God help us!" or "The ladies, God bless them!"; who rebuked without querulousness and praised without condescension; who took their questions and arguments seriously; who never mapped out their sphere for them, never urged them to be feminine or jeered at them for being female; who had no axe to grind and no uneasy male dignity to defend; who took them as he found them and was completely unselfconscious. There is no act, no sermon, no parable in the whole Gospel that borrows its pungency from female perversity; nobody could possibly guess from the words and deeds of Jesus that there was anything "funny" about woman's nature.

But we might easily deduce it from His contemporaries, and from His prophets before Him, and from His Church to this day. . . .

—Dorothy Sayers, 1890–1957

Sayers's intellectual writings included thoughtful treatises on theological questions of the time. This selection is from *Unpopular Opinions: Twenty-one Essays.*

~

MAMA

Yes—death done come in this here house. Done come walking in my house. On the lips of my children. You—what supposed to be my beginning again. You—what supposed to be my harvest. You—you mourning your brother?

BENEATHA

He's no brother of mine.

MAMA

What you say?

BENEATHA

I said that that individual in that room is no brother of mine.

MAMA

That's what I thought you said. You feeling like you is better than he is today? Yes? What you tell him a minute ago? That he wasn't a man? Yes? You give him up for me? You done wrote his epitaph too—like the rest of the world? Well, who give you the privilege?

BENEATHA

Be on my side for once! You saw what he just did, Mama! You saw him—down on his knees. Wasn't it you who taught me—to despise any man who would do that? Do what he's going to do?

MAMA

Yes—I taught you that. Me and your daddy. But I thought I taught you something else too—I thought I taught you to love him.

BENEATHA

Love him? There is nothing left to love.

MAMA

There is always something left to love. And if you ain't learned that, you ain't learned nothing. Have you cried for that boy today? I don't mean for yourself and the family 'cause we lost the money. I mean for him; what he been through and what it done to him. Child, when do you think is the time to love somebody the most; when they done good and made things easy for everybody? Well then, you ain't through learning—because that ain't the time at all. It's when he's at his lowest and can't believe in hisself 'cause the world done whipped him so. When you starts measuring somebody, measure him right, child, measure him right. Make sure you done taken into account what hills and valleys he come through before he got to wherever he is.

—*Lorraine Hansberry, 1930–1965*

Lorraine Hansberry was the first African American woman to write a major Broadway play, *A Raisin in the Sun,* which began performances in 1959 with the unknown Sidney Poitier in a leading role. She was 29 years old when the play opened. The play, from which this excerpt was taken, also became a movie.

~

[O] God, I have indeed transgressed your commandments. I have been impatient in reverses and trials. I am unsympathetic and unmerciful. I do not help my neighbor. I am unable to resist sin. I do not tire of doing wrong. Dear [God], pour out your grace to me and give me your Holy Spirit so that I may be obedient and keep each of your commandments. Help me to be at odds with the world and to give my heart and soul to you. Amen.

—*Martin Luther, 1483–1546;* alt.

Martin Luther, the Great Reformer, wrote a monumental translation of Scripture into the German vernacular so that ordinary people could read it, a feat that became a great contribution to literature for hundreds of years.

~

Lord, I have fallen again—a human clod!
Selfish I was, and heedless to offend;
Stood on my rights. Thy own child would not send
Away his shreds of nothing for the whole God!
Wretched, to thee who savest, low I bend:
Give me the power to let my rag-rights go
In the great wind that from thy gulf doth blow.

'Tis that I am not good—that is enough;
I pry no farther—that is not the way.
Here, O my potter, is thy making stuff!
Set thy wheel going; let it whir and play.
The chips in me, the stones, the straws, the sand,
Cast them out with fine separating hand,
And make a vessel of thy yielding clay.

—*George Macdonald, 1824–1905*

Scottish novelist and poet George Macdonald, who died in poverty, became known to a wider public when author C. S. Lewis credited his writings with having enabled Lewis to return to Christianity. This selection is from *Diary of an Old Soul.*

~

If there will be a third world war,
A war that will be won by losers
Losers winning everything but their life,
it's Life of greed.

If East and West shall never agree,
And negotiations drag on and on
While wars drain their coffers,
it's Life of greed.

If the North shall grow richer and richer,
And the South poorer and poorer,
it's Life of greed.

If millionaires conceive billionaires,
And beggars crowd the earth with paupers,
it's Life of greed.

If Christians build cathedrals for pianos huge and large,
And fellow believers can't buy a Bible,
it's Life of greed.

If two people occupy a six room house,
While four spend a winter night in the street below,
Christ must surely die again!
To enliven consciences buried in greed.

—*Tshenuwani Simon Farisani*

The Rev. Dr. T. Simon Farisani is a member of the South African parliament, representing his district in Venda, where for years he served both as dean and as bishop's deputy of the Lutheran Church. He was tortured and banned for his community service work while under apartheid. This selection is from his book *Justice in My Tears,* 1988.

~

The age of specialization doesn't work very well. One of the problems in this society is that the things that work in the short term don't work in the long term. There's a parable I like to use for this. You've probably heard of the Iditarod, the dog sled race across Alaska—people driving sleds pulled by dogs for more than a thousand miles. It lasts nearly two weeks. It is a long haul as races go, and for the last three years, it's been won by a woman named Susan Butcher. How is it that she has won? She says that her chief competitor starts his dogs early and drives them hard, and they get tired at the end of the day. So every day, he forges ahead of her, and at the end of the day his dogs are getting tired, and she's catching up. She wins the race essentially by not exploiting her dogs, by not exhausting them. Now, if the race only lasted two days, he would always win. If the race lasted a week, he would always win. But the race is long enough so that the caring and protection that she lavishes on her dogs turns into a winning strategy.

Now you see, we have organized our society so that the winning strategies are the short-term ones. We take presidents who care about the future, and we turn them into crisis managers. We lose the possibility of long-term, thoughtful leadership. Whether it's corporations and how they handle their budgets and the fact that their quarterly reports have to please the buyers for big pension funds and so on, or whether it's industry or labor or politics or [journalism] . . .

We have taught ourselves not to think in terms of the long haul, but the long haul is what lies between now and a decent life for our grandchildren. I've been looking at how women organize their lives and their careers. Sometimes I think that as more women come into full participation at higher policy levels, we may get more of this kind of long-term thinking. This is a moment of opportunity for a change in which we emphasize our public life.

—Mary Catherine Bateson

Anthropologist Bateson's books range from the social consequences of the AIDS epidemic to life with her celebrated parents, Margaret Mead and Gregory Bateson. This selection is from a television interview with Bill Moyers in 1988.

~

O God of earth and altar,
Bow down and hear our cry,
Our earthly rulers falter,
Our people drift and die;
The walls of gold entomb us,
The swords of scorn divide,
Take not your thunder from us,
But take away our pride!
From all that terror teaches,
From lies of tongue and pen,
From all the easy speeches,
That comfort cruel men,
From sale and profanation
Of honor and the sword,
From sleep and from damnation,
Deliver us, good Lord.

—G. K. Chesterton, 1874–1936

British journalist Gilbert Keith Chesterton made his living writing his mind on almost any topic with opinions favoring orthodox Roman Catholicism.

~

A Church which was not clear on the point of having a duty to this nation in need, and not merely the task of giving Christian instruction in direct form, but which has the task of making this Christian instruction known in words which grapple with the problems of the day—a Church which was not filled with anxiety to discover this word, would *a priori* betake itself to a corner of the graveyard. . . .

[Humankind] is a whole and can only exist as such a whole.

—*Karl Barth, 1886–1968;* alt.

Barth was a Swiss Reformed pastor and theologian. This selection is from *Dogmatics in Outline,* 1959.

~

O God, great champion of the outcast and the weak, we remember before you the people of other nations who are coming to our land seeking bread, a home, and a future. May we look with your compassion upon those who have been drained and stunted by the poverty and oppression of centuries, and whose minds have been warped by superstition or seared by the dumb agony of revolt.

We bless you for all that America has meant to the alien folk that have crossed the sea in the past, and for all the patient strength and God-fearing courage with which they have enriched our nation. We rejoice in the millions whose lives have expanded in the wealth and liberty of our country, and whose children have grown to fairer stature and larger thoughts; for we, too, are the children of immigrants who came with anxious hearts and halting feet on the westward path of hope.

—*Walter Rauschenbusch, 1861–1918*

Rauschenbusch was a seventh-generation minister and first-generation American among his German ancestors. His first parish was near Hell's Kitchen in New York City. This selection is from his book *Prayers of the Social Awakening,* 1925.

~

God of grace and God of glory,
On thy people pour thy power,
Crown thine ancient-church's story,
Bring its bud to glorious flower.
Grant us wisdom, Grant us courage,
For the facing of this hour.

Lo! the hosts of evil round us
Scorn thy Christ, assail your ways!
From the fears that long have bound us,
Free our hearts to faith and praise.
Grant us wisdom, Grant us courage,
For the living of these days.

Cure thy children's warring madness,
Bend our pride to thy control,
Shame our wanton, selfish gladness,
Rich in things and poor in soul.
Grant us wisdom, Grant us courage,
Lest we miss your peaceful goal.

—*Harry Emerson Fosdick, 1878–1969*

Renowned preacher Fosdick taught at Union Theological Seminary in New York City from 1915 to 1946. He wrote this hymn for the opening service and dedication of New York's Riverside Church, where he served for twenty years.

~

Nothing that is worth doing can be achieved
in our lifetime;
therefore we must be saved by hope.
Nothing which is true or beautiful or good makes
complete sense in any immediate context of history;
therefore we must be saved by faith.
Nothing we do, however virtuous, can be
accomplished alone;
therefore we are saved by love.
No virtuous act is quite as virtuous from the standpoint
of our friend or foe as it is from our standpoint.
Therefore we must be saved by the final form of love
which is forgiveness.

—*Reinhold Niebuhr, 1892–1971*

A towering theological presence in American Protestantism, Niebuhr taught at Union Seminary the concept of "Christian realism" that undergirded preachers through times of war. This selection is from *The Irony of American History.*

~

Chorus [While a Te Deum *is sung in Latin by a choir in the distance]:*

Forgive us, O Lord, we acknowledge ourselves as
type of the common man,
Of the men and women who shut the door and sit
by the fire;
Who fear the blessing of God, the loneliness of the night
of God, the surrender required, the deprivation inflicted;
Who fear the injustice of men less than the justice of God;

Who fear the hand at the window, the fire in the thatch,
  the fist in the tavern, the push into the canal,
Less than we fear the love of God.
We acknowledge our trespass, our weakness, our fault;
    we acknowledge
That the sin of the world is upon our heads; that the blood
  of the martyrs and the agony of the saints
Is upon our heads.
Lord, have mercy upon us.
Christ, have mercy upon us.
Lord, have mercy upon us.
Blessed Thomas, pray for us.

—*T. S. Eliot, 1888–1964*

American-born Thomas Stearns Eliot became a British subject in 1927. His play *Murder in the Cathedral,* 1935, was about the murder of Archbishop Thomas à Becket for opposing Henry II. This selection is from that play.

~

God made sun and moon to distinguish seasons and
  day and night.
And we cannot have the fruits of the earth but
  in their seasons,
But God hath made no decree to distinguish the
  seasons of mercy.

In paradise the fruits were ripe the first minute and
  in heaven it is always autumn;
God's mercies are ever in their maturity—

God never says you should have come yesterday.
God never says you must come again tomorrow;
    but today, if you will hear God's voice,
    today God will hear you—

God brought light out of darkness not out of lesser light.
God can bring thy summer out of winter though thou
  have no spring—

All occasions invite God's Mercies and all Times
  are God's Seasons.

—*John Donne, 1573–1631;* alt.

A convert from Catholicism to Anglicanism, Donne took holy orders and became a priest and one of England's greatest metaphysical poets.

III

"Love Your Neighbor As Yourself"

The Call to Care for Others

We the people of the United States, in order to form
a more perfect union, establish justice, insure domestic tranquility,
provide for the common defense, promote the general welfare,
and secure the Blessings of Liberty to ourselves and
our posterity, do ordain and establish this
Constitution for the United States of America.

—From Preamble to U.S. Constitution, 1788

One of the most significant psychological truths in the Bible is contained in Jesus' words to "love your neighbor as yourself." We cannot love our families let alone our neighbors if we cannot love and accept ourselves. Reaching out to care for others begins with the conviction that God cares for us and forgives our failings. We are worthy persons, valued by our Creator. From this position of confidence, we are freed from self concerns and can invest ourselves in others.

Americans are known abroad for their eternal optimism and "can do" spirit. We have shamelessly exploited our natural resources and we continue to live with the evils of racism and sexism and mindless consumerism, but we also believe we can do better—and that can make all the difference. The readings that follow can help us focus on what is involved in serving the common good, in loving our neighbors as ourselves.

May we unite in most humbly offering our prayers
and supplications
To the Great Ruler of Nations,
And to beseech God to pardon our national and
other transgressions;
To enable us all, whether in public or private stations,
To perform our several and relative duties properly
and punctually;
To render our national government a blessing to
all the people
By constantly being a government of wise,
just and constitutional laws,
Discreetly and faithfully executed and obeyed;
To protect and guide all sovereigns and nations,
And to bless them with good governments, peace and
concord;
To promote the knowledge and practice of true
religion and virtue,
And, generally, to grant unto all people such a degree
of temporal prosperity
As God alone knows to be best.

—*George Washington, 1732–1799;* alt.

President Washington belonged to a Church of England congregation in Virginia and wrote many prayers during his careers as a general of the Revolutionary Army and as president.

~

We hold these truths to be self-evident, that all . . . are created equal. That they are endowed by their Creator with certain inalienable rights, that among these are life, liberty and the pursuit of happiness. . . .

—*From Preamble to Declaration of Independence, 1776;* alt.

On July 4, 1776, delegates to the Continental Congress voted to accept the formal wording of the Declaration of Independence from Great Britain for the American colonies in the New World.

~

Then God spoke all these words:

I am the Lord your God, who brought you out of the land of Egypt, out of the house of slavery; you shall have no other gods before me.

You shall not make for yourself an idol, whether in the form of anything that is in heaven above, or that is on the earth beneath, or that is in the water under the earth.

You shall not bow down to them or worship them; for I the Lord your God am a jealous God, punishing children for the iniquity of parents, to the third and the fourth generation of those who reject me, but showing steadfast love to the thousandth generation of those who love me and keep my commandments.

You shall not make wrongful use of the name of the Lord your God, for the Lord will not acquit anyone who misuses his name.

Remember the sabbath day, and keep it holy. Six days you shall labor and do all your work. But the seventh day is a sabbath to the Lord your God; you shall not do any work—you, your son or your daughter, your male or female slave, your livestock, or the alien resident in your towns. For in six days the Lord made heaven and earth, the sea, and all that is in them, but rested the seventh day; therefore the Lord blessed the sabbath day and consecrated it.

Honor your father and your mother, so that your days may be long in the land that the Lord your God is giving you.

You shall not murder.

You shall not commit adultery.

You shall not steal.

You shall not bear false witness against your neighbor.

You shall not covet your neighbor's house; you shall not covet your neighbor's wife, or male or female slave, or ox, or donkey, or anything that belongs to your neighbor.

—*Exodus 20:1–18*

The story of Moses coming down from Mount Sinai to give God's Ten Commandments to the people of Israel is one of the most powerful in all of biblical history for both Jews and Christians. These rules for righteous living have guided people for millennia.

~

Almighty God, Who has given us this good land for our heritage; We humbly beseech Thee that we may always prove ourselves a people mindful of Thy favor and glad to do Thy will. Bless our land with honorable ministry, sound learning, and pure manners.

Save us from violence, discord, and confusion, from pride and arrogance, and from every evil way. Defend our liberties, and fashion into one united people the multitude brought hither out of many kindreds and tongues.

Endow with Thy spirit of wisdom those to whom in Thy name we entrust the authority of government, that there may be justice and peace at home, and that through obedience to Thy law, we may show forth Thy praise among the nations of the earth.

In time of prosperity fill our hearts with thankfulness and in the day of trouble, suffer not our trust in Thee to fail; all of which we ask through Jesus Christ our Lord. Amen.

—*Thomas Jefferson, 1743–1826*

The third president of the newly formed United States of America, Jefferson proclaimed a day of prayer for the nation in 1805. His contribution is called "A National Prayer for Peace."

~

A certain heathen came to Shammai and said to him, "Make me a proselyte, on condition that you teach me the whole Torah while I stand on one foot." Thereupon he repulsed him with the rod which was in his hand. When he went to Hillel, he said to him, "What is hateful to you, do not do to your neighbor: That is the whole Torah; all the rest of it is commentary; go and learn."

—*Talmud, Shabbat 31a*

Hillel lived near the end of the last century B.C.E. and the first century C.E. He was a preeminent Jewish teacher who founded the basic principles of biblical (Torah) interpretation. The Talmud is the authoritative body of Jewish tradition.

~

We utterly deny all outward wars and strife, and fightings with outward weapons, for any end, or under any pretense whatsoever: this is our testimony to the whole world. . . . The Spirit of Christ, by which we are guided, is not changeable, so as once to command us from a thing as evil, and again to move unto it; and we certainly know, and testify to the world, that the spirit of Christ, which leads us into all truth, will never move us to fight and war against any [one] with outward weapons, neither for the Kingdom of Christ nor for the kingdoms of this world. . . . Therefore, we cannot learn war any more.

—*Declaration from Society of Friends, 1660;* alt.

The Quakers have been known throughout their history as pacifists. This formal declaration to England's King Charles is a founding document of this policy. Its last sentence is used on peace banners throughout the world.

~

When the Pharisees heard that he [Jesus] had silenced the Sadducees, they gathered together, and one of them, a lawyer, asked him a question to test him. "Teacher, which commandment in the law is the greatest?" He said to him, "You shall love the Lord your God with all your heart, and with all your soul, and with all your mind. This is the greatest and first commandment. And a second is like it: 'You shall love your neighbor as yourself.' On these two commandments hang all the law and the prophets."

—*Matthew 22:34–40*

~

Tsekung asked, "Is there one word that can serve as a principle of conduct for life?" Confucius replied, "It is the word *shu*—reciprocity: Do not do to others where [sic] you do not want them to do to you."

—*Confucian* Analects *15.23*

Confucius, 551–479 B.C.E., is renowned as a philosopher, educator, social planner, and advocate of a philosophy for harmonious living and social transformation. His teachings undergird many of the cultures of Asia.

~

There are eight degrees in the giving of *tsedakah* (charity), one higher than the other.

1. Those who give grudgingly, reluctantly, or with regret.
2. Those who give less than is fitting, but give graciously.
3. Those who give what is fitting, but only after being asked.
4. Those who give before being asked.
5. Those who give without knowing to whom, although the recipients know the identity of the donors.
6. Those who give without making their identity known to the recipients.
7. Those who give without knowing to whom, and neither do the recipients know from whom they receive.
8. Those who help others by giving a gift or loan, or by making them business partners or finding them employment, thereby helping them dispense aid to others. . . . This means strengthening them in such a manner that falling into want is prevented.

—*Moses Maimonides, 1135–1204*

Revered scholar of the Torah, Spanish-born Maimonides is best known for his commentaries on the Mishna from the Talmud. This selection comes from Maimonides' *Eight Degrees of Tsedakah regarding Gifts to the Needy,* 10.

~

Whoever loves God, loves his works. Now the works of God are noble virtues. Therefore, whoever loves God, loves virtue. This love is true and full of consolation. It is virtue which proves the presence of love, not sweetness of devotion, for it sometimes happens that those who love less, feel more sweetness. But it is not according to what we feel that love is measured, but according to the extent that we are grounded in charity and rooted in love.

—*Hadewijch of Brabant, ca. 1204–1244*

Hadewijch of Brabant in Europe was a Beguine, a laywoman who chose a life of service without becoming a nun. In her visions, Hadewijch sees love as her God, a lady mistress who leads her through sufferings and gives joy and peace.

~

I sought for the key to the greatness and genius of America in her harbors . . . ; in her fertile fields and boundless forests; in her rich mines and vast world commerce; in her public school system and institutions of learning. I sought for it in her democratic Congress and in her matchless Constitution.

Not until I went into the churches of America and heard her pulpits flame with righteousness did I understand the secret of her genius and power.

America is great because America is good, and if America ever ceases to be good, America will cease to be great. . . .

The safeguard of morality is religion, and morality is the best security of law as well as the surest pledge of freedom.

—*Alexis de Tocqueville, 1805–1859*

Tocqueville from France toured America from 1851 to 1852 and recorded his impressions in *The Republic of the United States of America and Its Political Institutions, Reviewed and Examined,* from which this selection was taken.

~

Christ has no body now on earth but yours, no hands but yours, no feet but yours; yours are the eyes through which to look at Christ's compassion to the world, yours are the feet with which he is to go about doing good, and yours are the hands with which he is to bless us now.

—*St. Teresa of Avila, 1515–1582*

A Spanish woman of some wealth, Teresa experienced the presence of God with such power that her life was transformed. She founded the strict enclosure order of Carmelites and combined mysticism with a practical life of reform.

~

Love the saints of every faith;
Put away thy pride;
Remember, the essence of religion
Is meekness and sympathy,
Not fine clothes,

Not the Yogi's garb and ashes,
Not the blowing of the horn,
Not the shaven head,
Not long prayers,
Not recitations and torturings,
Not the ascetic way,
But a life of goodness and purity,
Amid the world's temptations.

—*Guru Nanak, 1469–1538*

The founder of Sikhism in India some five hundred years ago, Guru ("spokesperson for God") Nanak experienced a religious revelation that led him to teach that one's life should reflect a mindfulness of God in all daily activities.

~

With bended knees,
with hands outstretched,
do I yearn for the effective expression
of the holy spirit working within me:
For this love and understanding,
truth and justice;
for wisdom to know the apparent
from the real that I might alleviate
the sufferings of [people] on earth. . . .

God is love, understanding,
wisdom and virtue.
Let us love one another,
let us practice mercy and forgiveness,
let us have peace,
born of fellow-feeling. . . .

Let my joy be of altruistic living,
of doing good to others.
Happiness is unto [the one]
from whom happiness proceeds
to any other human being.
Response
We will practice what we profess.

—*A Zoroastrian Prayer*

Zoroastrianism is among the oldest of the monotheistic religions, dating from ca. 2000 B.C.E. Its founder, Zoroaster, lived on the East Iranian plateau. The primary sacred text is the Avestan, from which this prayer was taken.

~

Dear Sisters,

In the blessed unity in the Spirit of grace our Souls Salute you who are sanctified in Christ Jesus, and called to be Saints. . . . Where there is neither male nor female &c. but we are all one in Christ Jesus. . . .

And also Dear friends, in their womens monthly, and particular Meetings, that they take special care for the poore, and for those that stands in need: that there be no want, nor suffering, for outward things, amongst the people of God. . . .

And so let Care be taken for the poore, and widdows, that hath young Children, that they be relieved, and helped, till they be able and fitt, to be put out to apprentices or servants.

And that all the sick, and weak, and Infirme, or Aged, and widdows, and fatherless, that they be looked after, and helped, and relieved in every particular meeting, either with clothes, or maintenance, or what they stand in need of. So that in all things [God] may be glorified, and honoured, so that there be no want, nor suffering in the house of God, who loves a Chearfull giver. . . .

—*Margaret Fell, 1614–1702;* alt.

Margaret Fell was "the Mother of the Friends" in England who were committed to causes of social justice. This letter by Fell is from *Women's Speaking Justified, Proved and Allowed of by the Scriptures* sent to women in England and America.

~

O Lord, make me an instrument of Thy peace!
Where hate is, may I bring love;
Where offence has been given or taken, may I bring pardon;
Where there is discord, may I bring fellowship;
Where there is error, may I bring truth;
Where there is doubt, may I bring faith;
Where there is despair, may I bring hope;
Where there is darkness, may I bring light;
Where there is sadness, may I bring joy.

[O God], let me seek rather to console than to be consoled;
To understand than to be understood;
To love rather than to be loved;
For it is in giving that I receive,
In forgetting myself that I find myself;
In pardoning that I receive pardon;
In dying that I am born again to the life eternal.

—*Attributed to St. Francis of Assisi, 1181–1226*

This famous prayer is attributed most often to St. Francis, although some sources credit "L'Unioniste Romande" of France. A favorite text, it is widely used at meetings of Alcoholics Anonymous and other self-help groups.

~

The church is catholic, universal, as are all its actions; all that it does belongs to all. When it baptizes a child, that action concerns me; for that child is thereby connected to that head which is my head too, and ingrafted into that body whereof I am a member. And when it buries someone, that action concerns me: all of us are of one another, and are one volume. . . .

No [one] is an island, entire of itself, every one is a piece of the continent, a part of the main. If a clod be washed away by the sea, Europe is the less, as well as if a promontory were, as well as if a manor of thy friend's or of thine own were; any [one's] death diminishes me, because I am involved in [humankind]; and therefore never send to know for whom the bell tolls; it tolls for thee.

—*John Donne, 1573–1631;* alt.

Donne is considered one of the greatest of the seventeenth-century metaphysical poets. He also was dean of St. Paul's Cathedral in London and an eloquent preacher. This classic reading is from his book *Devotions upon Emergent Occasions.*

~

Not like the brazen giant of Greek fame,
With conquering limbs astride from land to land;
Here at our sea-washed, sunset gates shall stand

A mighty woman with a torch, whose flame
Is the imprisoned lightning, and her name
Mother of Exiles. From her beacon-hand
Glows world-wide welcome; her mild eyes command
The air-bridged harbor that twice cities frame.
"Keep, ancient lands, your storied pomp!" cries she
With silent lips. "Give me your tired, your poor,
Your huddled masses yearning to breathe free,
The wretched refuse of your teeming shore,
Send these, the homeless, tempest-tossed, to me;
I lift my lamp beside the golden door!

—*Emma Lazarus, 1849–1887*

This sonnet, "The Colossus," was inscribed on the base of the Statue of Liberty in 1883 to affirm America's welcome to new immigrants. A Russian Jewish immigrant herself, Lazarus became a poet in New York City.

~

The Settlement movement is only one manifestation of that wider humanitarian movement which throughout Christendom, but preeminently in England, is endeavoring to embody itself, not in a sect, but in society itself.

I believe that this turning, this renaissance of the early Christian humanitarianism, is going on in America, in Chicago, if you please, without leaders who write or philosophize, without much speaking, but with a bent to express in social service and in terms of action the spirit of Christ. Certain it is that spiritual force is found in the Settlement movement, and it is also true that this force must be evoked and must be called into play before the success of any

Settlement is assured. There must be the overmastering belief that all that is noblest in life is common to men and women, in order to accentuate the likenesses and ignore the differences which are found among the people whom the Settlement constantly brings into juxtaposition. . . .

In a thousand voices singing the Hallelujah Chorus in Handel's "Messiah," it is possible to distinguish the leading voices, but the differences of training and cultivation between them and the voices of the chorus are lost in the unity of purpose and in the fact that they are all human voices lifted by a high motive. This is a weak illustration of what a Settlement attempts to do. It aims, in a measure, to develop whatever of social life its neighborhood may afford, to focus and give form to that life, to bring to bear upon it the results of cultivation and training; but it receives in exchange for the music of isolated voices the volume and strength of the chorus.

—*Jane Addams, 1860–1935*

As a young and rather wealthy woman, Jane Addams became more interested in social reforms than in social pastimes. With friends she bought an old mansion in Chicago and turned it into a settlement house to provide services for poor people. Hull-House lasted more than a hundred years. She was awarded the Nobel Peace Prize in 1931.

~

It is far easier, though not very easy, to develop and preserve a spiritual outlook on life, than it is to make our everyday actions harmonise with that spiritual outlook. That means trying to see things, persons and choices from the angle of eternity; and dealing with them as part of the material in which the Spirit works.

This will be decisive for the way we behave as to our personal, social, and national obligations. It will decide the papers we read, the movements we support, the kind of administrators we vote for, our attitude to social and international justice. For though we may renounce the world for ourselves, refuse the attempt to get anything out of it, we have to accept it as the sphere in which we are to co-operate with the Spirit, and try to do the Will. Therefore the prevalent notion that spirituality and politics have nothing to do with one another is the exact opposite of the truth.

Once it is accepted in a realistic sense, the Spiritual Life has everything to do with politics. It means that certain convictions about God and the world become the moral and spiritual imperatives of our life; and this must be decisive for the way we choose to behave about that bit of the world over which we have been given a limited control.

—*Evelyn Underhill, 1875–1941*

Combining deep spirituality with academic excellence, British author and spiritual director Evelyn Underhill is best known for her devotional writings. Her major work is entitled *Mysticism,* a text still used today.

~

As we are together, praying for Peace, let us be truly with each other.
Silence
Let us pay attention to our breathing.
Silence

Let us be relaxed in our bodies and our minds.
Silence
Let us be at peace with our bodies and our minds.
Silence
Let us return to ourselves and become wholly ourselves. Let us maintain a half-smile on our faces.
Silence
Let us be aware of the source of being common to us all and to all living things.
Silence
Evoking the presence of the Great Compassion, let us fill our hearts with our own compassion—towards ourselves and towards all living things.
Silence
Let us pray that all living beings realize that they are all brothers and sisters, all nourished from the same source of life.
Silence
Let us pray that we ourselves cease to be the cause of suffering to each other.
Silence
Let us plead with ourselves to live in a way which will not deprive other living beings of air, water, food, shelter, or the chance to live.
Silence
With humility, with awareness of the existence of life, and of the sufferings that are going on around us, let us pray for the establishment of peace in our hearts and on earth. Amen

—*Thích Nhât Hanh*

A Buddhist monk from Vietnam, Thích Nhât Hanh is author of many devotional works, including *The Art of Mindful Living,* 1997.

~

The seeds of totalitarian regimes are nurtured by misery and want. They spread and grow in the evil soil of poverty and strife. They reach their full growth when the hope of a people for a better life has died. We must keep that hope alive. The free people of the world look to us for support in maintaining their freedom.

—*Harry S. Truman, 1884–1972*

The Truman Doctrine was a program of aid to the defeated nations of World War II. President Truman presented the plan in a speech to Congress on March 12, 1947, from which this selection was taken.

~

Father,
who has made all of us in thy likeness
and lovest all whom thou hast made,
suffer not our family to separate itself from thee
by building barriers of race and colour.
As thy Son our Saviour was born of a Hebrew mother, but
rejoiced in the faith of a Syrian woman and of a Roman
solider, welcomed the Greeks who sought him
and suffered a man from Africa to carry his cross,
so teach us to regard the members of all races as
fellow-heirs of the kingdom of Jesus Christ our Lord.

—*Toc H;* alt.

This selection is from *The Oxford Book of Prayer,* 1985.

~

I hate, I despise your festivals,
    and I take no delight in your solemn assemblies.
Even though you offer me your burnt offerings and
    grain offerings, I will not accept them;
    and the offerings of well-being of your fatted animals
    I will not look upon.
Take away from me the noise of your songs;
    I will not listen to the melody of your harps.
But let justice roll down like waters
    and righteousness like an ever-flowing stream.

—*Amos 5:21–24*

~

The Governments of the States Parties to this Constitution on behalf of their peoples declare:

That since wars begin in the minds of [human beings], it is in the minds of [human beings] that the defenses of peace must be constructed;

That ignorance of each other's ways and lives has been a common cause, throughout the history of [humankind], of that suspicion and mistrust between the peoples of the world through which their differences have all too often broken into war;

That the great and terrible war which has now ended was a war made possible by the denial of the democratic principles of the dignity, equality and mutual respect of [all peoples], and by the propagation, in their place, through ignorance and prejudice, of the doctrine of the inequality of races;

That the wide diffusion of culture, and the education of humanity for justice and liberty and peace are indispensable to the dignity of [human beings] and constitute a sacred duty which all the nations must fulfil in a spirit of mutual assistance and concern;

That a peace based exclusively upon the political and economic arrangements of governments would not be a peace which could secure the unanimous, lasting and sincere support of the peoples of the world, and that the peace must therefore be founded, if it is not to fail, upon the intellectual and moral solidarity of [humankind].

For these reasons, the States Parties to this Constitution, believing in full and equal opportunities for education for all, in the unrestricted pursuit of objective truth, and in the free exchange of ideas and knowledge, are agreed and determined to develop and to increase the means of communication between their peoples and to employ these means for the purposes of mutual understanding and a truer and more perfect knowledge of each other's lives. . . .

In consequence whereof they do hereby create the United Nations Educational, Scientific and Cultural Organization for the purpose of advancing, through the educational and scientific and cultural relations of the peoples of the world, the objectives of international peace and of the common welfare of [humankind] for which the United Nations Organization was established and which its Charter proclaims.

—*UNESCO Constitution;* alt.

UNESCO, the United Nations Education, Scientific, and Cultural Organization, was established in 1946. It seeks to broaden the base of education in the world, introduce scientific benefits to all people, and promote cultural interchange.

~

Our Democracy in this country had its roots in religious belief, and we had to acknowledge soon after its birth that differences in religious belief are inherent in the spirit of true Democracy. Just because so many beliefs flourished side by side, we were forced to accept the fact that "a belief" was important, but "what belief" was important only to the individual concerned. Later it was accepted that an individual in this land of ours had the right to any religion, or to no religion. The principle, however, of the responsibility of the individual for the well-being of neighbors which is akin to: "Love thy neighbor as thyself," in the New Testament, seems always to have been a part of the development of the Democratic ideal which has differentiated it from all other forms of government. . . . The motivating force of the theory of a Democratic way of life is still a belief that as individuals we live co-operatively, and, to the best of our ability, serve the community in which we live, and that our own success, to be real, must contribute to the success of others.

—*Eleanor Roosevelt, 1884–1962*

Frequently listed as among the greatest women of history, Eleanor Roosevelt was described as "the conscience of the New Deal" during her husband's presidential years. This excerpt is from her book *The Moral Basis of Democracy,* 1940.

~

God of justice,
you adorned the human race
with a marvelous diversity,
yet clothed each of its members
with a common dignity

that may never be diminished.
Put within us respect for that dignity
and a passion for the rights which flow from it,
that we may always champion for others
the justice we would seek for ourselves.
Grant this through our Lord Jesus Christ, your Son,
who lives and reigns with you in the unity of the
Holy Spirit,
God forever and ever.

—*Sacramentary*

This prayer was written for the International Commission on English in the Liturgy to include in a chapter entitled "Masses for Various Needs and Occasions" in its contemporary book of offices (services) of the church, *Sacramentary.*

~

People and their cultures perish in isolation, but they are born or reborn in contact with other men and women, with men and women of another culture, another creed, another race. If we do not recognize our humanity in others, we shall not recognize it in ourselves.

—*Carlos Fuentes*

The works of Mexican author and diplomat Fuentes, which include *Relations,* 1980, and *The Old Gringo,* 1985, are frequently translated. This selection was taken from *The Buried Mirror: Reflections on Spain and the New World.*

~

Just then a lawyer stood up to test Jesus. "Teacher," he said, "what must I do to inherit eternal life?" Jesus said to him, "What is written in the law? What do you read there?" The lawyer answered, "You shall love the Sovereign your God with all your heart, and with all your soul, and with all your strength, and with all your mind; and your neighbor as yourself." And Jesus said to him, "You have given the right answer; do this, and you will live."

But wanting to justify himself, the lawyer asked Jesus, "And who is my neighbor?" Jesus replied, "A man was going down from Jerusalem to Jericho, and fell into the hands of robbers, who stripped him, beat him, and went away, leaving him half dead. Now by chance a priest was going down that road; and when he saw him, he passed by on the other side. So likewise a Levite, when he came to the place and saw him, passed by on the other side. But a Samaritan while traveling came near him; and when he saw him, he was moved with pity. He went to him and bandaged his wounds, having poured oil and wine on them. Then he put him on his own animal, brought him to an inn, and took care of him. The next day he took out some money, gave it to the innkeeper, and said, 'Take care of him; and when I come back, I will repay you whatever more you spend.' Which of these three, do you think, was a neighbor to the man who fell into the hands of the robbers?" The lawyer said, "The one who showed him mercy." Jesus said to him, "Go and do likewise."

—*Luke 10:25–37*

~

a man who had fallen among thieves
lay by the roadside on his back
dressed in fifteenthrate ideas
wearing a round jeer for a hat

fate per a somewhat more than less
emancipated evening
had in return for consciousness
endowed him with a changeless grin

whereon a dozen staunch and leal
citizens did graze at pause
then fired by hypercivic zeal
sought newer pastures or because

swaddled with a frozen brook
of pinkest vomit out of eyes
which noticed nobody he looked
as if he did not care to rise
one hand did nothing on the vest
its wideflung friend clenched weakly dirt
while the mute trouserfly confessed
a button solemnly inert.

Brushing from whom the stiffened puke
i put him all into my arms
and staggered banged with terror through
a million billion trillion stars

—*E. E. Cummings, 1894–1962*

The hundreds of poems by E. E. (Edward Estlin) Cummings are easily recognized for their use of nonstandard punctuation—and for profound ideas in earthy verse. Cummings also wrote plays and novels.

~

In the ancient world of dictatorships, . . . individual acts of compassion were the only responses possible. In the modern industrial world of high technology, acts of compassion and justice become systemic. It would be useless for the Good Samaritan to ask for the HMO card from the man left for dead at the side of the road. In fact, in 20th century America, the Good Samaritan would be liable for a law suit if he moved the injured man. Tending to the health needs of all the people becomes a matter of universal health care, which in turn leads to highly political questions.

Individual personal acts of compassion are still needed. However, we are now confronted with a further application of the Gospel story of the Good Samaritan in the necessity of developing a universal health system, so that none will be left by the side of the road. These systems are needed as an expression of the Gospel, simply because of the immensity and complexity of the problems.

—*Don Benedict*

This selection was excerpted from "Closing Remarks Made to the Organizing Convention of Protestants for the Common Good" held at the Methodist Temple in Chicago, December 3, 1994. Don Benedict is co-coordinator of the organization.

~

In Germany they came first for the Communists, and I didn't speak up because I wasn't a Communist. Then they came for the Jews, and I didn't speak up because I wasn't a Jew. Then they came for the trade unionists, and I didn't speak up because I wasn't a trade unionist. Then they came for the Catholics, and I didn't speak up because I was a Protestant. Then they came for me, and by that time no one was left to speak up.

—*Martin Niemoeller, 1892–1984*

Niemoeller was pastor of a Reformed Church during the Nazi era in Germany and active with a group of clergy and lay friends in an underground "confessing church" that resisted National Socialism ideology.

~

I shall die, but that is all that I shall do for Death.
I hear him leading his horse out of the stall; I hear the
  clatter on the barn-floor.
He is in haste; he has business in Cuba, business
  in the Balkans, many calls to make this morning.
But I will not hold the bridle while he cinches the girth.
And he may mount by himself: I will not give him
  a leg up.

Though he flick my shoulders with his whip, I will not
  tell him which way the fox ran.
With his hoof on my breast I will not tell him where
  the black boy hides in the swamp.
I shall die, but that is all that I shall do for Death;
  I am not on his pay-roll.

I will not tell him the whereabouts of my friends
  nor of my enemies either.
Though he promise me much, I will not map him the
  route to any man's door.
Am I a spy in the land of the living, that I should
  deliver men to Death?
Brother, the password and the plans of our city are safe
  with me; never through me.
Shall you be overcome.

—*Edna St. Vincent Millay, 1892–1950*

Millay was born in Rockland, Maine, and graduated from Vassar. Her first long poem, "Renascence," was published when she was 19. She also has written plays and an opera libretto.

~

In judging our salvation or definitive damnation, God will not be guided by cultic criteria—when and how we prayed—not by doctrinal criteria—what truths we believe in. God will be guided by ethical criteria: what we did for others. The eternal destiny of human beings will be measured by how much or how little solidarity we have displayed with the hungry, the thirsty, the naked, and the oppressed. In the end we will be judged in terms of love.

—*Leonardo Boff*

Brazilian liberation theologian Boff is best known for his book *Jesus-Christ Liberator,* 1972. This selection is from his book *Way of the Cross, Way of Justice.*

~

A brother said to an old man: There were two brothers. One of them stays in his cell quietly, fasting for six days at a time, and imposing on himself a good deal of discipline, and the other serves the sick. Which one of them is more acceptable to God? The old man replied: Even if the brother who fasts six days were to hang himself by the nose, he could not equal the one who serves the sick.

—*From* Desert Wisdom, *1982*

The Eastern Orthodox tradition continues to use writings of the fourth-century Desert Fathers in its teachings and worship.

~

And the Blessed One observed the ways of society and noticed how much misery came from malignity and foolish offences done only to gratify vanity and self-seeking pride.

And the Buddha said: "If a [person] foolishly does me wrong, I will return to [that one] the protection of my ungrudging love; the more evil comes from [one], the more good shall go from me; the fragrance of goodness always comes to me, and the harmful air of evil goes to [evil-doers]."

A foolish man learning that the Buddha observed the principle of great love which commends the return of good for evil, came and abused him. The Buddha was silent, pitying his folly.

When the man had finished his abuse, the Buddha asked him, saying: "Son, if [someone]declined to accept a present . . . , to whom would it belong?" And he answered: "In that case it would belong to [the one] who offered it."

"My son," said the Buddha, "thou hast railed at me, but I decline to accept thy abuse, and request thee to keep it thyself. Will it not be a source of misery to thee? As the echo belongs to the sound, and the shadow to the substance, so misery will overtake the evil-doer without fail."

The abuser made no reply, and Buddha continued:

"A wicked [one] who reproaches a virtuous one is like one who looks up and spits at heaven; the spittle soils not the heaven, but comes back and defiles [the spitter's] own person.

"The slanderer is like one who flings dust at another when the wind is contrary; the dust does but return on [the one] who threw it. The virtuous [one] cannot be hurt and the misery that the other would inflict comes back on [oneself]."

The abuser went away ashamed, but he came again and took refuge in the Buddha, the Dharma, and the Sangha.

—*Shakyamuni (Buddha), 500 B.C.E.;* alt.

The Buddhist "Way of Virtue" is presented in English in the work entitled *The Dhammapadad: The Gospel of Buddha,* 1915, edited by Paul Caros, from which this selection was taken.

~

For the church, the many abuses of human life, liberty and dignity are a heartfelt suffering. The church, entrusted with the earth's glory, believes that in each person is the Creator's image and that everyone who tramples it offends God. As the holy defender of God's rights and of God's images, the church must cry out. It takes as spittle in its face, as lashes on its back, as the cross in its passion, all that human beings suffer, even though they be unbelievers. They suffer as God's images.

There is no dichotomy between humans and God's image. Whoever tortures a human being, whoever abuses a human being, whoever outrages a human being abuses God's image, and the church takes as its own that cross, that martyrdom.

—*Oscar Arnulfo Romero, 1917–1980*

El Salvadoran archbishop and human rights advocate Romero was assassinated by government agents while celebrating mass. Some of his words were collected in a work entitled *The Church Is All of You,* 1984.

~

The most important work to help our children is done quietly—in our homes and neighborhoods, our parishes and community organizations. No government can love a child and no policy can substitute for a family's care, but clearly families can be helped or hurt in their irreplaceable roles. Government can either support or undermine families as they cope with the moral, social, and economic stresses of caring for children.

There has been an unfortunate, unnecessary, and unreal polarization in discussions of the best way to help families. Some emphasize the primary role of moral values and personal responsibility, the sacrifices to be made and the personal behaviors to be avoided, but often ignore or deemphasize the broader forces which hurt families, e.g., the impact of economics, discrimination, and antifamily policies. Others emphasize the social and economic forces that undermine families and the responsibility of government to meet human needs, but they often neglect the importance of basic values and personal responsibility.

The undeniable fact is that our children's future is shaped both by the values of their parents and the policies of our nation.

—*National Conference of Catholic Bishops, 1991*

This excerpt is from *Putting Children and Families First: A Challenge for Our Church, Nation, and World,* a pastoral letter first distributed in November 1991.

~

The greatest threat to our national security and future comes from no external enemy but from the enemy within—in our loss of strong, moral, family, and community values and support. Parent by parent, youth by youth, voter by voter, professional by professional, congregation by congregation, club by club, community by community, foundation by foundation, corporation by corporation, city by city, county by county, state by state—all Americans must commit personally and as voters to a national crusade of conscience and action that will ensure that no child is left behind. Only we—individually and collectively—can transform our nation's priorities and assure its future as we face a new century and begin a new millennium.

—*Marian Wright Edelman*

Head of the Children's Defense Fund, Edelman was raised in a family of devout Christians. She collected writings on moral virtue from her own and her husband's Jewish tradition for a book entitled *The Measure of Our Success: A Letter to My Children and Yours,* from which this excerpt was taken.

~

I had the most extraordinary experience of love of neighbor with a Hindu family. A gentleman came to our house and said: "Mother Teresa, there is a family who have not eaten for so long. Do something." So I took some rice and went there immediately. And I saw the children—their eyes shining with hunger. I don't know if you have ever seen hunger, but I have seen it very often. And the mother of the family took the rice I gave her and went out. When she came back, I asked her: "Where did you go? What did you do?" And she gave me a very simple answer: "They are hungry also." What struck me was that she knew—and who are they? A Muslim family—and she knew. I didn't bring any more rice that evening because I wanted them, Hindus and Muslims, to enjoy the joy of sharing.

But there were those children, radiating joy, sharing the joy and peace with their mother because she had the love to give until it hurts. And you see, this is where love begins—at home in the family.

So, as the example of this family shows, God will never forget us and there is something you and I can always do. We can keep the joy of loving Jesus in our hearts, and share that joy with all we come in contact with. Let us make that one point—that no child will be unwanted, unloved, uncared for, or killed and thrown away. And give until it hurts—with a smile.

—*Mother Teresa, 1910–1997*

Beloved founder and leader emeritus of the Sisters of Charity stationed in Calcutta, India, Mother Teresa received the Nobel Peace Prize in 1979. This selection is from her speech entitled "Whatever You Did unto One of the Least, You Did unto Me" delivered at the National Prayer Breakfast, 1994, in Washington, D.C.

~

The infinite joy of touching the Godhead is easily attained by those who are free from the burden of evil and established within themselves. They see the Self in every creature and all creation in the Self. With consciousness unified through meditation, they see everything with an equal eye. . . .

When [we] respond to the joys and sorrows of others as if they were [our] own, [we have] attained the highest state of spiritual union.

—*Bhagavad-gītā 6:28–32;* alt.

The Bhagavad-gītā is the essence of India's ancient Vedic wisdom and one of the great spiritual and philosophical classics of the world. It is written in the form of a battlefield dialogue between the Lord Krishna, Supreme Personality of Godhead, and Arjuna, his friend and disciple.

~

It is in your hands to form new generations, to lead them in the right directions, to instill into them those principles which are the seed of good works, though for the moment they may seem hidden. The impressions of children are never obliterated. We shall be indebted to you, if the youth whom you educate, when grown up, become the pride of the family and society, of the state and of the church. . . .

—*St. Frances Xavier Cabrini, 1850–1917*

Mother Cabrini and a group of missionary sisters from Italy landed in the United States in 1889. During her lifetime they opened schools, orphanages, and hospitals in eight U.S. states and in seven foreign countries.

~

I appeal to you therefore, brothers and sisters, by the mercies of God, to present your bodies as a living sacrifice, holy and acceptable to God, which is your spiritual worship. Do not be conformed to this world, but be transformed by the renewing of your minds, so that you may discern what is the will of God—what is good and acceptable and perfect. . . .

Let love be genuine; hate what is evil, hold fast to what is good; love one another with mutual affection; outdo one another in showing honor. Do not lag in zeal, be ardent in spirit, serve the Lord. Rejoice in hope, be patient in suffering, persevere in prayer. Contribute to the needs of the saints; extend hospitality to strangers.

Bless those who persecute you; bless and do not curse them. Rejoice with those who rejoice, weep with those who weep. Live in harmony with one another; do not be haughty, but associate with the lowly; do not claim to be wiser than you are. Do not repay anyone evil for evil, but take thought for what is noble in the sight of all. . . .

Do not be overcome by evil, but overcome evil with good.

—*Romans 12:1–2, 9–17, 21*

~

Almighty God, who hast given us this good land for our heritage; We humbly beseech thee that we may always prove ourselves a people mindful of thy favour and glad to do thy will. Bless our land with honorable industry, sound learning, and pure manners. Save us from violence, discord, and confusion; from pride and arrogancy, and from every evil way.

Defend our liberties, and fashion into one united people the multitudes brought hither out of many kindreds and tongues. Endue with the spirit of wisdom those to whom in thy Name we entrust the authority of government, that there may be justice and peace at home, and that, through obedience to thy law, we may show forth thy praise among the nations of the earth.

In the time of prosperity, fill our hearts with thankfulness and in the day of trouble, suffer not our trust in thee to fail; all which we ask through Jesus Christ our Lord. Amen.

—*The Book of Common Prayer*

The Book of Common Prayer first came into use on Whitsunday, 1549, replacing the service books of the breviary, missal, and manual. It was revised in 1662. This prayer is from a 1979 edition.

~

Almighty God, as we stand here at this moment, my future associates in the executive branch of government join me in beseeching that Thou will make full and complete our dedication to the service of the people in this throng, and their fellow citizens everywhere.

Give us, we pray, the power to discern clearly right from wrong, and allow all our words and actions to be governed thereby, and by the laws of this land. Especially we pray that our concern shall be for all the people regardless of station, race, or calling.

May cooperation be permitted and be the mutual aim of those who, under the concepts of our Constitution, hold to differing political faiths; so that all may work for the good of our beloved country and Thy glory. Amen.

—*Dwight David Eisenhower, 1890–1969*

President Eisenhower gave this prayer on the occasion of his inauguration in 1953.

~

Take all hate from my heart, O God, and teach me how to take it from the hearts of others. Open my eyes and show me what things in our society make it easy for hatred to flourish and hard for us to conquer it. Then help me to try to change these things.

And so open my eyes and my ears that I may this coming day be able to do some work of peace for Thee.

—*Alan Paton, 1903–1988*

Born in Pietermaritzburg, Natal, South Africa, Paton was a teacher and educational administrator and later leader of a political party while writing many books about the evils of apartheid. His books include the devotional book *Instrument of Thy Peace,* from which this selection was taken.

~

My purpose alone must be God's purpose—to increase the welfare and happiness of [God's] people. Nature will not permit a vacuum. It will be filled with something.

Human need is really a great spiritual vacuum which God seeks to fill. . . .

With one hand in the hand of a [neighbor] in need and the other in the hand of Christ, [God] could get across the vacuum and I became an agent. Then the passage, "I can do all things through Christ which strengtheneth me," comes to have real meaning.

—*George Washington Carver, ca. 1864–1943;* alt.

Carver, an African American botanist of international fame, introduced hundreds of uses for the peanut, soybean, pecan, and sweet potato. This selection is from *Carver of Tuskegee* by Ethel Edwards.

~

In those early days we were often asked why we had come to live on Halsted Street when we could afford to live somewhere else. I remember one man who used to shake his head and say it was "the strangest thing he had met in his experience," but who was finally convinced that it was "not strange but nature." In time it came to seem natural to all of us that the Settlement should be there. If it is natural to feed the hungry and care for the sick, it is certainly natural to give pleasure to the young, comfort to the aged, and to minister to the deep-seated craving for social intercourse that all [people] feel. Whoever does it is rewarded by something which, if not gratitude, is at least spontaneous and vital and lacks that irksome sense of obligation with which a substantial benefit is too often acknowledged.

In addition to the neighbors who responded to the receptions and classes, we found those who were too battered and oppressed to care for them. To these, however, was left that susceptibility to the bare offices of humanity which raises such offices into a bond of fellowship.

From the first it seemed understood that we were ready to perform the humblest neighborhood services. We were asked to wash the newborn babies, and to prepare the dead for burial, to nurse the sick, and to "mind the children."...

Perhaps these first days laid the simple human foundations which are certainly essential for continuous living among the poor: first, genuine preference for residence in an industrial quarter to any other part of the city, because it is interesting and makes the human appeals; and second, the conviction ... that the things which make [us] alike are finer and better than the things that keep [us] apart, and that these basic likenesses, if they are properly accentuated, easily transcend the less essential differences of race, language, creed and tradition.

Perhaps even in those first days we made a beginning toward that object which was afterwards stated in our charter: "To provide a center for a higher civic and social life; to institute and maintain educational and philanthropic enterprises, and to investigate and improve the conditions in the industrial districts of Chicago."

—*Jane Addams, 1860–1935;* alt.

Founder of Chicago's famed social service institution Hull-House, Jane Addams spent her life serving the poor in the city. This selection is taken from an article by Addams in *One Hundred Years at Hull-House.*

~

The poor must know that we love them, that they are wanted. They themselves have nothing to give but love. We are concerned with how to get this message of love and compassion across. We are trying to bring peace to the world through our work. But the work is the gift of God, eh? . . .

Love can be misused for selfish motives. I love you, but at the same time I want to take from you as much as I can, even the things that are not for me to take. Then there is no true love any more. True love hurts. It always has to hurt. It must be painful to love someone, painful to leave them, you might have to die for them. When people marry they have to give up everything to love each other. The mother who gives birth to her child suffers much. It is the same for us in religious life. To belong fully to God we have to give up everything. Only then can we truly love. The word "love" is so misunderstood and so misused.

A young American couple told me once, "You know a lot about love; you must be married." And I said, "Yes, but sometimes I find it difficult to smile at Him."

—*Mother Teresa, 1910–1997*

Friend and author Desmond Doig followed the saintly Mother Teresa as she carried out her duties at the mission station in Calcutta and then recorded her words in a book entitled *Mother Teresa: Her People and Her Work,* 1976. This excerpt is from that text.

~

O God—when I have food,
Help me to remember the hungry;
When I have work,
Help me to remember the jobless;
When I have a warm home,
Help me to remember the homeless;
When I am without pain,
Help me to remember those who suffer;
And remembering,
Help me to destroy my complacency,
And bestir my compassion.
Make me concerned enough to help,
By word and deed, those who cry out—
For what we take for granted. Amen.

—*Anonymous*

~

Love, of course, means something much more than mere sentiment, much more than token favours and perfunctory almsdeeds. . . . The fact is that good done to another as to an object is of little or no spiritual value. Love takes one's neighbour as one's other self, and loves [the neighbor] with all the immense humility and discretion and reserve and reverence without which no one can presume to enter into the sanctuary of another's subjectivity. From such love all authoritarian brutality, all exploitation, domineering and condescension must necessarily be absent.

—*Thomas Merton, 1915–1968;* alt.

Merton was born in France and taught at Columbia University. A convert to Roman Catholicism, Merton joined the Trappist order at Our Lady of Gethsemane Abbey, Kentucky, in 1941. This selection is from *The Wisdom of the Desert,* 1968.

~

Krishnamurti and Patwardhan were important to me precisely because they were what Christians might call "witnesses" to their faith; they somehow embodied their faith in their lives. In retrospect, it is somewhat embarrassing to articulate this as a discovery, but as a twenty-year-old it came as news to me: Christians did not have a corner on love, wisdom, and justice. Christians were not the only ones nourished by faith and empowered by their faith to work to change the world. I knew nothing of the Hindu devotional traditions of *bhakti* then, but I met people—like Krishnamurti and Patwardhan—whose very lives were a message of God-grounded love. These people, unbeknownst to them, pushed me into a life of work and inquiry, spiritual and intellectual. I became a student of comparative religion and focused my work on Hinduism and the traditions of India. And as a Christian I began to realize that to speak of Christ and the meaning of incarnation might just mean being radically open to the possibility that God really encounters us in the lives of people of other faiths. . . .

The meeting of Banaras and Bozeman, "East and West," can be duplicated in a hundred keys and a hundred languages.

The encounter of worlds and worldviews is the shared experience of our times. We see it in the great movements of modern history, in colonialism, and the rejection of colonialism, in the late-twentieth-century "politics of identity"—ethnic, racial, and religious. We experience our own personal versions of this encounter, all of us, whether Christian, Hindu, Jewish, or Muslim; whether Buddhist, Apache, or Kikuyu; whether religious, secular, or atheist. What do we make of the encounter with a different world, a different worldview? How will we think about the heterogeneity of our immediate world and our wider world? This is our question, our human question, at the end of the twentieth century.

—*Diana Eck*

Professor of Indian studies and comparative religion at Harvard, Diana Eck is currently directing a project to document the spiritual diversity of America. In this excerpt from her 1993 book *Encountering God: A Spiritual Journey from Bozeman to Banaras,* she credits two East Indian friends from Banaras, India, with opening her eyes to the power of other religious traditions. Her hometown is Bozeman, Montana.

~

Eternal God, whose image lies in the hearts of all people,
We live among peoples whose ways are different from ours,
whose faiths are foreign to us,
whose tongues are unintelligible to us.
Help us to remember that you love all people with
your great love,
that all religion is an attempt to respond to you,
that the yearnings of other hearts are much like
our own and are known to you.

Help us to recognize you in the words of truth,
the things of beauty, the actions of love about us.
We pray through Christ, who is a stranger to no one
land more than another, and to every land no less
than to another.

—*Robert H. Adams Jr.*

This prayer, written by Adams for *A Traveler's Prayer Book,* was used at the Vancouver Assembly of the World Council of Churches in 1983.

~

We must remember the suffering of my people, as we must remember that of the Ethiopians, the Cambodians, the boat people, the Palestinians, the Mesquite Indians, the Argentinian desaparecidos—the list seems endless.

Let us remember Job, who, having lost everything—his children, his friends, his possessions, and even his argument with God—still found the strength to begin again, to rebuild his life. Job was determined not to repudiate the creation, however imperfect, that God had entrusted to him.

—*Elie Wiesel*

A survivor of the Holocaust, Wiesel was given the Nobel Peace Prize in 1986 for his tireless efforts to defend victims of inhumanity everywhere. This excerpt is from his acceptance address.

~

People are people—strike them, and they will cry; cut them, and they will bleed; starve them, and they will wither away and die.

But treat them with respect and decency, give them equal access to the levers of power, attend to their aspirations and grievances, and they will flourish and grow and, if you will excuse an ungrammatical phrase, join together "to form a more perfect union."

—*Thurgood Marshall, 1908–1993*

As chief counsel of the NAACP, Marshall led the team that won the landmark suit before the Supreme Court in 1954 against the doctrine of "separate but equal" education for African Americans. He became a Supreme Court Justice himself in 1967.

~

[The one] who regards
With an eye that is equal
Friends and comrades,
The foe and the [kin],
The vile, the wicked,
[Those] who judge [us],
And those who belong
To neither faction:
[That one] is the greatest.

—*Bhagavad-gītā;* alt.

Here Lord Krishna teaches his friend Arjuna about the science of self-realization or Vedic knowledge, a philosophy thousands of years old and recorded in the many translations of this classic text.

~

To approach the black . . . struggle against the white . . . racism as a human problem, I said we had to forget hypocritical politics and propaganda. I said that both races, as human beings, had the obligation, the responsibility, of helping to correct America's problem. The well-meaning white people . . . had to combat, actively and directly, the racism in other white people. And the black people had to build within themselves much greater awareness that along with equal rights there had to be the bearing of equal responsibilities.

—*Malcolm X, 1925–1965*

Malcolm was six years old when his preacher father was killed by a white mob, his mother suffered a nervous breakdown, and he and his siblings were sent to foster homes. After a conversion in prison, Malcolm became a leader of the Nation of Islam. This excerpt is from *The Autobiography of Malcolm X* by Alex Haley, published shortly after Malcolm's assassination by rivals.

~

While my personal life has been filled with momentous crises and upheavals throughout the years I have lived in this country, by the grace of God I have done well professionally. I am now a professor and chairperson of the Religious Studies Program at the University of Louisville. My specialization is in the area of Islamic Studies, and it was due to this expertise that I became involved in various ways, and at various levels, in the discussions going on around the country regarding Islam, after the Arab oil embargo of 1973 and the Iranian revolution of 1979 convinced the Western world that Islam was a living reality in the world.

While I found many of these discussions, in which I was called upon to explain "Islamic revival" to Americans, interesting and stimulating, it was in another setting—that of interreligious dialogue among believers in the one God—

that I found the community of faith I had sought all my life. In this community of faith I have found others who, like myself, are committed to creating a new world in which human beings will not brutalize or victimize one another in the name of God, but will affirm, through word and action, that as God is just and loving so human beings must treat each other with justice and love regardless of sex, creed, or color. I have found in my community of faith what I did not find in my community of birth: the possibility of growing and healing, of becoming integrated and whole.

Due to the affirmation I have received from men and women of faith, I am no longer the fragmented, mutilated woman that I once was. I know now that I am not alone in the wilderness, that there are some people in the world who understand my calling, and that their prayers are with me as I continue my struggle on behalf of the millions of nameless, voiceless, faceless Muslim women of the world who live and die unsung, uncelebrated in birth, unmourned in death.

—*Riffat Hassan*

Born and raised in Pakistan, Hassan went to school in England. She began her study of women's issues in Islam after moving to the United States with her young daughter, where she has become the leading feminist scholar of the *Qur'an*. This excerpt is from "Jihād Fī Sabīl Allah: A Muslim Woman's Faith Journey from Struggle to Struggle to Struggle," 1991.

~

How beautiful will be the day when all the baptized understand that their work, their job, is a priestly work, that just as I celebrate Mass at the altar, so each carpenter celebrates Mass at the workbench, and each metalworker, each professional, each doctor with the scalpel, the market woman at her stand, are performing a priestly office!

How many cabdrivers I know listen to this message there in their cabs; you are a priest at the wheel, my friend, if you work with honesty, consecrating that taxi of yours to God, bearing a message of peace and love to the passengers who ride in your cab.

—*Oscar Arnulfo Romero, 1917–1980*

Archbishop Romero of El Salvador fought against the injustices of the rulers of his country until they assassinated him. This excerpt is from his book *The Violence of Love,* 1988, translated by James R. Brockman.

~

The glory of God, the splendor, the fullness of God—I prefer to translate this mysterious word with "the beauty of God." To be comforted does not mean that we receive something, a thing, an object from God but that we catch sight of the beauty and splendor of God. Where, then, do we see that? What can we find that?

The Bible is quite clear on this point. The beauty, the splendor of God is visible in all those who prepare God's way. The messianic work of liberation awaits us. God entrusts us with preparing the way of the Messiah. God does not say to anyone, "You are just a simple housewife or a mere employee and understand nothing of complicated necessities." Prepare the way of God, comfort the people in their weakness, make them into street workers on God's way. No man is too small or too large, no woman is too young or too old, too educated or too ignorant. God has given all of us a part, God comforts us, and we prepare God's way. God's voice calls to us and we answer. God's spirit wants to make us courageous and capable of truth. God wants to be born in us.

—*Dorothee Soelle*

A German theologian, feminist, and social activist, Soelle has written numerous books. She taught at Union Theological Seminary in New York City from 1975 to 1987. This excerpt is from *Theology for Skeptics,* 1995.

~

The joint, as Fats Waller would have said, was jumping. . . . And, during the last set, the saxophone player took off on a terrific solo. He was a kid from some insane place like Jersey City or Syracuse, but somewhere along the line he had discovered he could say it with a saxophone. He stood there, wide-legged, humping the air, filling his barrel chest, shivering in the rags of his twenty-odd years, and screaming through the horn, "Do you love me?" "Do you love me?" "Do you love me?" And again—"Do you love me?" "Do you love me?" "Do you love me?" The same phrase unbearably, endlessly, and variously repeated with all the force the kid had. . . .

The question was terrible and real. The boy was blowing with his lungs and guts out of his own short past; and somewhere in the past, in gutters or gang fights . . . in the acrid room, behind marijuana or the needles, under the smell in the precinct basement, he had received a blow from which he would never recover, and this no one wanted to believe. Do you love me? Do you love me? Do you love me? The men on the stand stayed with him cool and at a little distance, adding and questioning. . . . But each man knew that the boy was blowing for every one of them. . . .

—*James Baldwin, 1924–1987*

Raised in a strict religious home, Baldwin became a preacher at the age of 14. He spent ten years in Paris, where he wrote *Go Tell It on the Mountain,* 1953, his first major work. Thereafter his home was New York City. This excerpt is from *Another Country,* 1960.

~

The life of this planet, and especially its human life, is a life in which something has gone wrong, and badly wrong. Every time that we see an unhappy face, an unhealthy body, hear a bitter or despairing word, we are reminded of that.

The occasional dazzling flashes of pure beauty, pure goodness, pure love which show us what God wants and what [God] is, only throw into more vivid relief the horror of cruelty, greed, oppression, hatred, ugliness; and also the mere muddle and stupidity which frustrate and bring suffering into life. Unless we put on blinkers, we can hardly avoid seeing all this; and unless we are warmly wrapped up in our own cozy ideas, and absorbed in our own interests, we surely cannot help feeling the sense of obligation, the shame of acquiescence, the call to do something about it.

To say day by day "Thy Kingdom Come"—if these tremendous words really stand for a conviction and desire—does not mean "I quite hope that some day the Kingdom of God will be established, and peace and goodwill prevail. But at present I don't see how it is to be managed or what I can do about it." On the contrary, it means, or should mean, "Here am I! Send me!"—active, costly collaboration with the Spirit in whom we believe.

—*Evelyn Underhill, 1875–1941;* alt.

An Anglican mystical poet and writer, Underhill became a lecturer on the philosophy of religion at Oxford. Her many books included *The Spiritual Life,* from which this selection was taken.

~

Let the word go forth from this time and place, to friend and foe alike, that the torch has been passed to a new generation of Americans.

Let every nation know, whether it wishes us well or ill, that we shall pay any price, bear any burden, meet any hardship, support any friend, oppose any foe, to assure the survival and the success of liberty.

Now the trumpet summons us again—not as a call to bear arms, though arms we need; not as a call to battle, though embattled we are; but a call to bear the burden of a long twilight struggle, a struggle against the common enemies of [humankind]: tyranny, poverty, disease, and war itself.

In the long history of the world, only a few generations have been granted the role of defending freedom in its hour of maximum danger. I do not shrink from this responsibility—I welcome it.

The energy, the faith, the devotion which we bring to this endeavor will light our country and all who serve it—and the glow from that fire can truly light the world.

And so, my fellow Americans, ask not what your country can do for you: ask what you can do for your country.

My fellow citizens of the world: ask not what America will do for you, but what together we can do for the freedom of [humankind].

With a good conscience our only sure reward, with history the final judge of our deeds, let us go forth to lead the land we love, asking [God's] blessing and [God's] help, but knowing that here on earth God's work must truly be our own.

—*John F. Kennedy, 1917–1963;* alt.

The youngest person and the first Roman Catholic ever elected president of the United States, Kennedy supported a "New Frontier" in social legislation. The excerpt comes from his inaugural address, 1961, parts of which are engraved on his tomb in Arlington National Cemetery.

~

O Thou who compassest the whole earth with Thy most merciful favour and willest not that any of Thy children should perish, I would call down Thy blessing today upon all who are striving towards the making of a better world. I pray, O God, especially—

—for all who are valiant for truth;
—for all who are working for purer and juster laws;
—for all who are working for peace between the nations;
—for all who are engaged in healing disease;
—for all who are engaged in the relief of poverty;
—for all who are engaged in the rescue of the fallen;
—for all who are working towards the restoration of the broken unity of Thy Holy Church;
—for all who preach the gospel;

—for all who bear witness to Christ in foreign lands;
—for all who suffer for righteousness' sake.

Cast down, O Lord, all the forces of cruelty and wrong. Defeat all selfish and worldly-minded schemes, and prosper all that is conceived among us in the spirit of Christ and carried out to the honour of [Your] blessed name. Amen.

—*John Baillie, 1886–1960;* alt.

Scottish theologian and cleric Baillie taught at Auburn and Union seminaries in New York between 1920 and 1935. His eloquent book *A Diary of Private Prayer,* 1949, from which this prayer was taken, is still used throughout the world.

~

The most eloquent prayer is the prayer through hands that heal and bless. The highest form of worship is the worship of unselfish Christian service. The greatest form of praise is the sound of consecrated feet seeking out the lost and helpless.

—*Billy Graham*

William Franklin "Billy" Graham is a world-renowned evangelist and friend of U.S. presidents. This statement was given to *The Chicago American* in 1967.

~

A man once asked the Prophet what was the best thing in Islam, and the latter replied, "It is to feed the hungry and to give the greeting of peace both to those one knows and to those one does not know."

—*Hadīth of Bukhārī*

Islam has several sources of the teachings of the Prophet Muhammad, including the Qur'an and the "Sunnah" or "Hadith"—sayings, actions, and approvals of the Prophet. This statement is from *Muhammad and the Islamic Tradition,* 1974.

~

Thus says the Lord: Act with justice and righteousness, and deliver from the hand of the oppressor anyone who has been robbed. And do no wrong or violence to the alien, the orphan, and the widow, or shed innocent blood in this place.

—*Jeremiah 22:3*

~

People talk about imitating Jesus Christ, and imitate him in the little trifling, formal things, such as washing the feet, saying his prayer, and so on, but if anyone attempts a real imitation, there are no bounds to the outcry with which the presumption of that person is condemned.

For instance, Jesus was saying something to the people one day, which interested him very much, and interested them very much, and Mary and his brothers came in the middle of it, and wanted to interrupt him, and take him home to dinner, very likely—(how natural that story is! does it not speak more home than any historic evidences of the Gospel's reality?), and he, instead of being angry with their interruption of him in such all important work for some trifling thing, answers, "Who is my mother? and who are my brethren? Whosoever shall do the will of my Father which is in heaven, the same is my brother and sister and mother." But if we were to say that, we should be accused of "destroying the family tie, of diminishing the obligation of the home duties."

He might well say, "Heaven and earth shall pass away, but my words shall not pass away." His words will never pass away. If he had said, "Tell them that I am engaged at this moment in something very important; that the instruction of the multitude ought to go before any personal ties; that I will remember to come when I have done," no one would have been impressed by his words; but how striking is that, "Behold my mother and my brethren!"

—*Florence Nightingale, 1820–1910*

Florence Nightingale's wealthy British family was horrified when she began devoting her life to caring for the sick, especially war victims. Her bravery on the Crimean War front is legendary. This selection is from her book *Cassandra*.

~

When I pick up a person from the street hungry, I give [that person] a plate of rice, a piece of bread; I have satisfied. I have removed that hunger. But a person who is shut out, who feels unwanted, unloved, terrified, the person who has been thrown out from society—that poverty is so full of hurt and so unbearable, and I find that very difficult.... And so let us always meet each other with a smile, for the smile is the beginning of love, and once we begin to love each other naturally we want to do something.

—*Mother Teresa, 1910–1997*

The beloved founder of the Missionaries of Charity in India, Mother Teresa was known as the "Saint of Calcutta" for her works of mercy in its slums. This selection is from her Nobel Peace Prize address in 1979.

~

Our duties are kindness towards all creatures, patience, humility, truth, purity, contentment, decorum of manners, gentleness of speech, friendliness, freedom from envy or avarice and the habit of speaking evil of others.

— *Vishnu*

This selection is a saying from Hindu scripture, "Ancient Tales of Vishnu," dating from an early century C.E. Vishnu is one of the Holy Trinity of Hindu dieties.

~

When we had managed the stairs
they stank of urine and garbage
joe limps toward us
an old man twice as thin as I
he had been reading a religious book
but difficult words like colossians and circumcision
he didn't know and he looked them up in his bible
his eyes are weak

as we sit with him a while
I hear that he is only forty-four
but drugs and alcohol have not
left much of him remaining
he chain smokes and whistles through a white tube
that extends out of his throat.
He tells of his great aunt in georgia
he would like to be at her burial there
he speaks of the plants he would like to have
a few for spring and then one

that blooms in summer and then these permanent ones
the apartment is bare two hand towels hang
from the clothesline across the middle of the
    room the children
from the building paid him a visit afterward
the radio was gone

In case he drinks again his heart
won't be able to handle it in case the
food stamps for the poor
are done away with in the interest of an ordered
balance sheet
he won't eat anything more.

My student and friend the pale baptist
prays for him and for us
and give joe he says to god what he needs
and above all your kingdom.

—*Dorothee Soelle*

Entitled "On a visit among the poor in the glitter of Manhattan," this poem is from Soelle's book *Theology for Skeptics,* 1995. She lives and works in Hamburg, Germany.

~

Both [people] of science and [people] of art live always at the edge of mystery, surrounded by it; both always, as the measure of their creation, have had to do with the harmonization of what is new with what is familiar, with the balance between novelty and synthesis, with the struggle to make partial order in total chaos. They can, in their work and in their lives, help themselves, help one another, and help all [people]. They can make the paths that connect the villages of arts and sciences with each other and with the world at large the multiple, varied, precious bonds of a true and world-wide community.

This cannot be an easy life. We shall have a rugged time of it to keep our minds open and to keep them deep, to keep our sense of beauty and our ability to make it, and our occasional ability to see it in places remote and strange and unfamiliar; we shall have a rugged time of it, all of us, in keeping these gardens in our villages, in keeping open the manifold, intricate, casual paths, to keep these flourishing in a great, open, windy world; but this, as I see it, is the condition of [humankind]; and in this condition we can help, because we can love, one another.

—*J. Robert Oppenheimer, 1904–1967;* alt.

Famed leader of the project to develop the atomic bomb during World War II, Julius Robert Oppenheimer later taught in California and at Princeton. This selection is from his book entitled *The Open Mind,* 1955.

~

One result of the stimulation of your intellectual life that takes place in college is usually a shrinking of the imaginative life. This sounds like a paradox, but I have often found it to be true. Students get so bound up with difficulties such as reconciling the clashing of so many different faiths such as Buddhism, Mohamedanism, etc., that they cease to look for God in other ways. Bridges once wrote Gerard Manley Hopkins and asked him to tell him how he, Bridges, could believe. Bridges was an agnostic. He must have expected from Hopkins a long philosophical answer. Hopkins wrote back, "Give alms." He was trying to say to Bridges that God is to be experienced in Charity (in the sense of love for the divine image in human beings). Don't get so entangled with intellectual difficulties that you fail to look for God in this way.

—*Flannery O'Connor, 1925–1964*

Georgia-born O'Connor is described as "the finest short-story writer of her generation." This selection is from a collection of her letters entitled *The Habit of Being,* 1979.

~

As a mother with her own life guards the life of her own child, let all-embracing thoughts for all that lives be thine.

—*Buddhist Teaching*

Reverence for all life is central to Buddhist teachings. This selection is from *Kuddaka Patha,* 1960, Bhikkhu Nanamoli, translator.

~

You must teach your children that the ground between their feet is the ashes of our ancestors. So that they will respect the land, tell your children that the earth is rich with the lives of our kin. Teach your children what we have taught our children, that the earth is our mother. Whatever befalls the earth befalls the children of the earth.

This we know. The earth does not belong to us; we belong to the earth. This we know. All things are connected like the blood which unites one family. All things are connected. Whatever befalls the earth befalls the children of the earth. We do not weave the web of life, we are merely a strand in it. Whatever we do to the web, we do to ourselves.

—*Attributed to Chief Seattle, 1786–1866*

It is uncertain that this excerpt came from an address by Chief Seattle of the Suquamish and Duwamish tribes at an assembly before white settlers in 1854. A translation of the speech by a pioneer who heard it was published in a Seattle newspaper thirty years later. However, through repeated use over years it has become accepted as his by Indian groups who say it represents Native American beliefs then and now.

~

Loving Savior and Ever Present Friend, we thank you this morning for the opportunity to pray for ourselves and for others. We know that no prayer goes unanswered. We trust you, Lord, and we love you. We know that you will be steadfast—Oh thank you, Jesus.

We acknowledge that our hearts are heavy because the truth of the Gospel is as yet squandered. Some of your poor children are not yet listening; some pathetic souls are unable to hear; and others are simply unwilling to comply. And so we pray this morning for those who are spiritual paupers:

- Persons who are destitute, penniless, without the necessities to sustain a home, or a table, or a bed. [Please] motivate us to share all that we have with those who have nothing.

- Persons whose very souls are impoverished—lacking in love, showing no kindness—compel us to reach out to these scrooged persons, loving them into humanness.

We pray for the poor persons who are only able to find comfort in the hollow pleasures of hedonism. Oblige us away from envy, and toward the setting of an example of righteous living.

We pray for the needy persons whose barren imaginations [are] cracked and splintered. Entreat us to risk challenging them. Teaming with them, let us dare to cooperate into your vision.

We pray for the destitute persons who are trapped in the violence of stalking and slaying victims as an acceptable occupation. Turn bystander mentality into tangible acts of justice at any price.

Lord, there are depleted persons who selfishly never take time for renewal [while] seeking to be indispensable. Teach us how to quiet their raging egos, and to give healing balm to the wounds of low self-esteem.

We pray for those who do shoddy work in their jobs because they feel unvalued, unseen, disrespected. Grant that we who are their co-workers may no longer tolerate being shortchanged.

O Lord, we pray this morning as poor people—knowing that ours is the kingdom of God. You promised that the poor in spirit shall be filled; that the poor shall laugh (Luke 6:20–21). We thank you and we rejoice!

In all the complexity of living, grant us simplicity to love those who are our enemies. Let us do good [while] hoping for nothing in return. In all the power struggles, family member to family member, city to city, nation to nation, help us realize that the greatest power is shown not in might, but in selflessness.

Lord, there are people in our church community who

need your tender mercy. . . . We ask you to bless each of them. We ask that you bless their families and those who care for them. We ask that you energize our church to surround the poor and the needy with love and attention, and the kind of faith that heals, and redeems, and transforms lives.

All these things we ask in the name of Jesus who listens to all trials; who in our distress kindly helps us.

—*Nancy Lynne Westfield*

This prayer by Pastor Westfield was given in November 1993 at Riverside Church in New York.

~

. . . by helping those who suffer physically
to overcome physical suffering,
those who are in fear to overcome fear,
those who suffer mentally to overcome mental suffering,
Be of service to all living beings.

—*Siddhārtha Gautama, the Buddha, ca. 563–483* B.C.E.

Entitled "The Welfare of All," this reading is quoted in *Dharma World,* July/August 1992.

~

We live in a way of life that is destroying the globe, socially, economically and ecologically. Can we lose that life so that we might find a life more in accord with the will of God? That is not an idealistic appeal. It is a statement of hard realism. Judgment for our ways is closing in on us. Never have Moses' words in his final challenge to the children of

Israel when he said that the choice before us is life or death been more apt than today. . . .

For the truth of our condition is that we are not isolated atoms, bits of matter in motion, motivated only by self-interest, real only in the privacy of our deep selves but alien to both nature and other human beings. Those metaphors—a physicalistic cosmos composed of dead and meaningless matter, and an economistic understanding of human motivation—surround us and reinforce a Gnostic innerness as the last refuge of meaning in an empty world.

The truth, if we can recover it, is much more adequately expressed in the biblical metaphor of creation, if we understand it as a mode of being rather than a quasi-scientific hypothesis about the origin of matter. For if everything that is is God's creation, then being as such is good (*esse, qua esse, bonum est*), as Saint Augustine said, then the cosmos is not empty, meaningless and dead, but full of meaning and value. Every squirrel, every tree, every rock, is God's creation and so calls forth our respect and concern. To blame a few lines in Genesis for our ecological crisis when the scriptures remind us again and again that the whole creation manifests the glory of God is a strange distortion, an expression of bad conscience, in my view, from those whose belief in a mechanistic cosmos gives a much more plausible excuse for its ruthless exploitation. With respect to other human beings, if we see them not only as created but as created in the image of God, no matter how distorted that image may have become, we are certainly more likely to respond to them with trust and love than if we view them essentially as competitors in a market economy that ultimately includes every sphere of life, even religion—the sphere of competition for market shares of believers. . . .

The attempted secession of our affluent classes into gated and guarded residential communities supposedly safe from the crumbling society around them is one expression of the Gnostic mentality. In such a situation it is not easy to be the church, not easy for Christians of any vocation, and I suspect especially not easy for ministers. While we certainly cannot claim to have all the answers to the enormous social and individual problems that confront us in America and the world, if it is true that the Kingdom of God is already among us, we can, through the renewal of our own religious communities, offer to the world what it most desperately needs.

—*Robert N. Bellah*

Sociology professor emeritus at the University of California in Berkeley, Bellah is co-author of the landmark book *Habits of the Heart,* 1985. This excerpt is from a speech entitled "Living Out the Ecumenical Vision in America Today" presented at a staff conference of the National Council of Churches in 1992.

~

What good is it, my brothers and sisters, if you say you have faith but do not have works? Can faith save you? If a brother or sister is naked and lacks daily food, and one of you says to them, "Go in peace, keep warm and eat your fill," and yet you do not supply their bodily needs, what is the good of that? So faith by itself, if it has no works, is dead.

—*James 2:14–17*

~

Relieve people in distress as speedily as you must release a fish from a dry rill [lest it die]. Deliver people from danger as quickly as you must free a sparrow from a tight noose. Be compassionate to orphans and relieve widows. Respect the old and help the poor.

—*Taoist Teaching*

Taoism derives its name from a book of wisdom, *Tao Te Ching* (Book of Tao and Virtue), originating in the sixth century B.C.E. This reading is from *Yin Chih Wen,* 1906, a work reflecting on the lessons of Taoism.

~

Liberation theology, feminist theology, and pluralist theology are all major currents in the Christian tradition today. All three are about the redefinition of the we in theological thinking and the renegotiation of the we in our common political and cultural life. They are all attempts to reconstruct more inclusive and more relevant forms of Christian thinking, Christian engagement. Liberation theologians articulate the Gospel as understood by the poor, the marginalized, those who speak the word of truth outside the houses of privilege and comfort and who insist that our priorities be set, not by the interests of the mighty, but by the priorities of the poor. Feminist theologians give voice to the concerns of both women and men who insist on the presence and perspective of women in Christian leadership, teaching, and interpretation. Pluralist theologians insist that Christians must also listen to the voices of people of other faiths and not pretend that we can do our theological and ethical thinking in a vacuum, without engaging in energetic interreligious exchange.

Unfortunately, there has not as yet been much interrelation between these three currents of theological thinking. Many Christians who speak of the "preferential option for the poor" seem not to recognize that most of the world's poor are not Christians who will speak the Gospel in a new prophetic voice—they are Muslim poor or Hindu poor. To hear their voices necessitates interreligious dialogue. Many of those who want to listen to the voices of Buddhists and Hindus pay scarcely any attention to the voices of women and reinforce in their interreligious dialogue the patriarchies of all the traditions; many who want to give voice to the perspectives of women within the Christian tradition don't think for a moment about Hindus and Buddhists. Everyone is busy on his or her own front. In a sense this is not a criticism, for feminist and womanist theologians, liberation theologians, and pluralist theologians have all, in their own ways, unleashed their respective revolutions in Christian thinking today. I believe, however, that we all must begin to think of these issues together, for I am convinced that they belong together as part of our effort to rebuild a sense of community that does not make difference divisive and exclusive.

—*Diana Eck*

A Harvard professor of religion and Indian studies, Eck believes all religions carry truths that can be appreciated. Her book *Encountering God,* from which this selection is taken, won the 1995 Louisville Grawemeyer Award in Religion.

~

We began to study the Bible as our main text. Many relationships in the Bible are like those we have with our ancestors, our ancestors whose lives were very much like our own. The important thing for us is that we started to identify that reality with our own. . . .

We Indians do not dream of great riches, we want only enough to live on. There is also the story of David, a little shepherd boy who appears in the Bible, who was able to defeat the king of those days, King Goliath. This story is the example for the children. This is how we look for stories and psalms which teach us how to defend ourselves from our enemies. I remember taking examples from all the texts which helped the community to understand their situation better. It's not only now that there are great kings, powerful men, people who hold power in their hands. Our ancestors suffered under them too. This is how we identify with the lives of our ancestors who were conquered by a great desire for power—our ancestors were murdered and tortured because they were Indians. We began studying more deeply and, well, we came to a conclusion. That being a Christian means thinking of our [people] around us, and that everyone of our Indian race has the right to eat. This reflects what God . . . said, that on this earth we have a right to what we need. The Bible was our principal text for study as Christians and it showed us what the role of a Christian is. . . .

For us the Bible is our main weapon. It has shown us the way. Perhaps those who call themselves Christians but who are really only Christians in theory, won't understand why we give the Bible the meaning we do. But that's because they haven't lived as we have. And also perhaps because they can't analyze it. I can assure you that any one of my community, even though . . . illiterate and . . . [needing] to have it read . . . and translated . . . , can learn many lessons from it, because . . . [no one] has difficulty understanding what reality is and what the difference is between the paradise up above, in Heaven, and the reality of our people here on Earth. We do this because we feel it is the duty of Christians to create the kingdom of God on Earth among our [people]. This kingdom will exist only when we all have enough to eat, when our children, brothers, parents don't have to die from hunger and malnutrition. That will be the "Glory," a Kingdom for we who had never known it. I'm only talking about the Catholic church in general terms because, in fact, many priests came to our region and were anti-communists, but nevertheless understood that the people weren't communists but hungry; not communists, but exploited by the system. And they joined our people's struggle too, they opted for the life we Indians live.

—*Rigoberta Menchu;* alt.

This selection is from *I, Rigoberta Menchu,* 1959, a book told by a Quiche Indian woman in Guatemala to anthropologist Elizabeth Burgos-Debray. In 1978, Menchu's brother, father, and mother were murdered by the army. Six of her nine brothers and sisters have disappeared. She fled to Mexico in 1981. When she won the Nobel Peace Prize in 1992, President Jorge Serrano scorned her award, calling it a victory for Guatemalan guerrillas.

~

Greater attention and resources must also be focused on the growing gap between the Northern and the Southern Hemispheres. A just and lasting peace will never be achieved when so many people live in abject poverty.

Peacemaking requires new forms of solidarity in the 1990s. Perhaps the bluntest way to put this message is the immorality of isolationism. After the Cold War, there is an understandable but dangerous temptation to turn inward, to focus only on domestic needs and to ignore our global responsibilities.

But this is not an option for believers in the universal church nor citizens in the world's last superpower. . . .

Building peace, securing democracy, confronting poverty and despair, and protecting human rights are not only moral imperatives but also wise national priorities. They can shape a world that will be a safer, more secure and more just home.

—Joseph Cardinal Bernardin, 1928–1996

As president of the National Conference of Catholic Bishops and the U.S. Catholic Conference, Cardinal Bernardin became known as a reconciler of conflicting positions among church leaders. He was archbishop of Chicago from 1982 until his death from cancer in 1996.

~

1. Let us be grateful for *kami's* (deity) grace and ancestors' benevolence and with bright and pure *makoto* (sincerity or true heart) perform religious services.
2. Let us work for people and the world, and serve as representatives of the kami to make the society firm and sound.
3. In accordance with the Emperor's will, let us be harmonious and peaceful and pray for the nation's development as well as the world's coexistence and co-prosperity.

—The General Principles of Shinto Life

This declaration was presented at the tenth anniversary of the founding of the Association of Shinto Shrines, 1956, and since that time has been recited at the beginning of many meetings of Shrine Shinto. The translator is Naofusa Hirai.

~

New York, February 23—When I hear it said that people in trouble aren't worth helping because if they had what it takes they wouldn't be in trouble, I like to remember the story of Sylvester Harris.

The delightful story of Harris is told in the March [1957] Ebony Magazine.

Harris, who lives on a farm at Columbus, Mississippi, is supposed to have ridden into town on his mule, Jesse, during the Depression and, according to legend, there put in a call to the President to ask help in saving his farm.

Harris says the truth of the story is that he did not ride his mule but got into an old truck which managed to get him into Columbus. He was told that the call to the President would cost him $4.80, so he stacked the nickels and quarters in front of him in the telephone booth and put in the call.

He got an assistant and a secretary, but he insisted on talking to the President. He was about to lose his mule and his farm and he would talk to no one else. Finally, he did get the President on the phone.

Two days later appraisers came and went over Harris's land, got him a government loan at the Federal Land Bank of New Orleans which satisfied his mortgage, and overnight he and his mule became a symbol of the "forgotten men" of that day.

Harris is 65 now and has a modern farm with a tractor,

cultivators and trailers. His old mule, Jesse, is dead but he has two new ones. His home has electricity, a refrigerator, a radio, a washing machine and two TV sets, and he cooks with gas.

A gentleman in Texas asked me the other day if giving economic aid to people in countries which do not seem able to get along by themselves has any value. I told him that without aid these people would go on being helpless, but with it we might see miracles occur. He looked very doubtful.

I wish now I had told him the story of Sylvester Harris.

—*Eleanor Roosevelt, 1884–1962*

After her husband's death in 1946, Eleanor Roosevelt became U.S. representative to the UN Assembly and chair of the UN Human Rights Commission. She also wrote a syndicated newspaper column entitled "My Day." This reading is from that column dated February 23, 1957.

~

When the human race neglects its weaker members, when the family neglects its weakest one—it's the first blow in a suicidal movement. I see the neglect in cities around the country, in poor white children in West Virginia and Virginia and Kentucky—in the big cities, too, for that matter. I see the neglect of Native American children in the concentration camps called reservations.

The powerful say, "Pull yourself up by your bootstraps." But they don't really believe that those living on denuded reservations, or on strip-mined hills, or in ghettos that are destinations for drugs from Colombia and Iraq, can somehow pull themselves up. What they're really saying is, "If you can, do, but if you can't, forget it." It's the most pernicious of all acts of segregation, because it is so subtle. . . .

We've made a lot of progress—it's dangerous not to say so. Because if we [don't] say so, we tell young people, implicitly or explicitly, that there can be no change. Then they compute: "You mean the life and death and work of Malcolm X and Martin King, the Kennedys, Medgar Evers, Fannie Lou Hamer, the life and struggle of Rosa Parks—they did all that and *nothing has changed?* Well, then, what the hell am I doing? There's no point for me to do anything." The truth is, a lot has changed—for the good. And it's gonna keep getting better, according to how we put our courage forward, and thrust our hearts forth.

—*Maya Angelou*

Celebrated poet and author Angelou came to national attention with the publication of her first autobiographical book, *I Know Why the Caged Bird Sings,* 1970. This excerpt is from an interview with Ken Kelley, a freelance writer, in a 1997 article for *Mother Jones.*

~

It is in the service of and guided by the vision of God's shalom that our various communities have been led to ministries of service and vocations of public advocacy in the past. Acting individually and sometimes together we have sought to provide food, shelter, child care, counseling, jobs programs, health clinics, elderly and disabled services, solace, succor and strength to neighbors in need. The involvement of our own vast networks of volunteers has taught us much about the extent of need in our society and of the dignity of those in need.

Together religious institutions have historically witnessed to the whole nation as a part of the exercise of religious freedom. Though such efforts must now be intensified, they can not substitute for just public policy reflective of the common good. That is why people of faith now have come to call for the establishment of policies, programs and governmental action that seek to secure justice and promote the general welfare. This religiously motivated commitment to the common good does not mean that we always find full unity in applying these principles on specific and complex matters of public policy. Rather, in the notion of shalom we find a common calling to action and advocacy which will be shared not only within but beyond our own communities.

—*National Council of the Churches of Christ, USA*
Synagogue Council of America
United States Catholic Conference

This excerpt is from "A Call to the Common Ground for the Common Good" issued in June 1993 by the three religious bodies.

~

We propel ourselves through these endless cycles, as if, after two hundred years of American education, we don't know what works and we are suddenly about to find out. Once we find out, of course, we'll share it with the poor. Baloney. We know what works. We're just not willing to pay the bill. Even President Bush knows Head Start works, but he says we don't have $5 billion to provide it for every child who needs it. But somehow we found $50 billion to restore the [emir] of Kuwait to his throne. Which is more important to [North] America?

—*Jonathan Kozol*

Social critic and author of numerous works analyzing America's schools and policies toward children, Kozol first came to public attention with his book entitled *Death at an Early Age: The Destruction of the Hearts and Minds of Negro Children in Boston Public Schools,* 1972. This excerpt is from an interview with him by Niki Amarantides that appeared in *The Other Side,* May–June 1992.

~

O Lord, teach us to humble ourselves before these children who live the gospel of love and drugs because we did not live the gospel of love. Teach us to humble ourselves before the problems that face our children in this generation. Especially we pray for all parents, that they may love their children steadfastly, even in the face of bewilderment and grief. Teach us to humble ourselves when we contemplate the world we have made, the millions that we have killed and maimed in the cause of justice. And above all make us the instruments of Your love, that we may love those who call out that they love us all. Even if we cannot help them, teach us to love them.

All this we ask in the name of God, who so loved the world, and of . . . Jesus, the lover of our souls.

—*Alan Paton, 1903–1988*

South African writer and educator, Paton gained world fame and local controversy with the publication of *Cry, the Beloved Country,* 1948, a story of interracial love in a time of apartheid. This prayer is from his small devotional book *Instrument of Thy Peace,* 1968.

~

All deeds are right in the sight of the doer,
    but the Lord weighs the heart.
To do righteousness and justice
    is more acceptable to the Lord than sacrifice.

—*Proverbs 21:2–3*

~

Once, as Rabbi Yohanan ben Zakkai was coming forth from Jerusalem, Rabbi Joshua followed after him and beheld the Temple in ruins.

"Woe unto us," Rabbi Joshua cried, "that this, the place where the iniquities of Israel were atoned for, is laid waste!"

"My son," Rabbi Yohanan said to him, "be not grieved. We have another atonement as effective as this. And what is it? It is acts of loving-kindness, as it is said, 'For I desire mercy and not sacrifice.' " (Hosea 6.6)

—*Talmud*

The vast collection of ancient teachings that make up the Talmud is second only to the Hebrew Bible in significance for Jews. This reading came from Abot de Rabbi Nathan 6, *Rabbinic Anthology.*

~

Some are of the opinion
That their success to love is great
So all the world blooms for them
And turns green.
But then we learn the truth
And see that it is not so:
For it is only our works of faithfulness
That prove our progress in love.

—*Hadewijch of Brabant, 1204–1244*

One of the early women mystics of the church, Hadewijch chose a life of devotion and service without the constraints of marriage or a cloistered order of the church. She became a writer of great devotional works.

~

Two men were fishing by a stream when an infant floated past. The first fisherman jumped in, rescued the child and handed him up to safety in the second fisherman's arms.

No sooner had they settled the child down on the grass when a second infant floated along. Again, the fishermen jumped in and rescued the baby. A third baby floated along, a fourth, and so on. The fishermen saved each in turn. Finally, a whole group of babies came floating downstream.

The first fisherman grabbed as many as he could and looked up to see his friend walking away. "Hey," he shouted, "what's wrong with you? Aren't you going to help me save these babies?" To which the second fisherman replied, "You save these babies. I'm going upstream to see who's throwing all those babies into the river!"

—*Folk Parable*

This version of a popular story that appears in many variations with the same point was taken from *America's Children at Risk: A National Agenda for Legal Action* prepared in 1993 by the American Bar Association.

~

I recently heard a story on the radio. It happened in Bosnia, but I think it has meaning for all of us. A reporter was covering that tragic conflict in the middle of Sarajevo, and he saw a little girl shot by a sniper. The back of her head had been torn away by the bullet. The reporter threw down his pad and pencil, and stopped being a reporter for a few minutes. He rushed to the man who was holding the child, and helped them both into his car.

As the reporter stepped on the accelerator, racing to the hospital, the man holding the bleeding child said, "Hurry, my friend, my child is still alive." A moment or two later, "Hurry, my friend, my child is still breathing." A moment later, "Hurry, my friend, my child is still warm." Finally, "Hurry. Oh my God, my child is getting cold."

When they got to the hospital, the little girl had died. As the two men were in the lavatory, washing the blood off their hands and their clothes, the man turned to the reporter and said, "This is a terrible task for me. I must go tell her father that his child is dead. He will be heartbroken."

The reporter was amazed. He looked at the grieving man and said, "I thought she was your child." The man looked back and said, "No, but aren't they all our children?"

Aren't they all our children?

Yes, they are all our children. They are also God's children as well, and he has entrusted us with their care in Sarajevo, in Somalia, in New York City, in Los Angeles, in my hometown of Perry, Georgia, and here in Washington, D.C.

—*Sam Nunn*

U.S. Senator Sam Nunn of Georgia was chair of the Senate Armed Services Committee from 1987 until 1995. This excerpt is from his address to the National Prayer Breakfast in Washington, D.C., February 1, 1996.

IV

"So That You Will Be a Blessing"

Gratitude for God's Gifts

From the delight of young animals in simply
being alive, from children at play, from youth risking all for love,
from the triumphs that follow long effort—from all these,
faith gathers materials for her Temple to form
a bulwark against the storm.

—Helen Keller, 1880–1968

The power to love faithfully and the courage to care meaningfully can only come from a thankful heart. When we contemplate what God has done for us—in the awesomeness of the cosmos, in the excitement of changing seasons, in the beauty of nature, in the love of family and friends, and in our own capacity to love in return—we praise and glorify our Creator and seek ways to show our gratitude.

We are the inheritors of God's word to Abraham so many millennia ago: "I will bless you . . . so that you will be a blessing . . . and in you all the families of the earth shall be blessed."

The passages that follow remind us of the well-springs of thankfulness that compel us to serve the common good.

It would have been enough
if You had simply given life to us,
O Genesis of Our Being,
but You also gave us meaning
and liberty
and love.
How shall we respond
to such an outpouring of blessing,
except to give back life for Life
and love for unending Love.
Amen.

—*Miriam Therese Winter*

A nun of the Medical Mission Sisters, Sr. Winter earned her Ph.D. in liturgical studies at Princeton in 1983. She has written many liturgical books and songs, including "A Mass of a Pilgrim People," which premiered in Carnegie Hall in 1967. This prayer is from her book *WomanWisdom,* 1991.

~

Good Heaven! any one thing in the creation is sufficient to demonstrate a Providence, to a humble and grateful mind. The mere possibility of producing milk from grass, cheese from milk, and wool from skins; who formed and planned it? Ought we not, whether we dig or plough or eat, to sing this hymn to God?

Great is God, who has supplied us with these instruments to till the ground; great is God, who has given us hands and instruments of digestion; who has given us to grow insensibly and to breathe in sleep. These things we ought forever to celebrate. . . .

But because the most of you are blind and insensible, there must be some one to fill this station, and lead, in behalf of all, the hymn to God; for what else can I do, a lame old man, but sing hymns to God? Were I a nightingale, I would act the part of a nightingale; were I a swan, the part of a swan. But since I am a reasonable creature, it is my duty to praise God . . . and I call on you to join the same song.

—*Epictetus, ca. 55–ca. 135* C.E.

Born a slave in Asia Minor at the beginning of the last millennium, Epictetus came to Rome, where he somehow obtained an education and eventually won his freedom. He became a respected teacher and Stoic philosopher.

~

O most high, almighty, good majestic God, to Thee belong
praise, glory, honour, and all blessing!
Praised be my Sovereign God with all Thy creatures;
and specially our brother the sun, who brings us the day,
and who brings us the light;
fair is he, and shining with a very great splendour:
O God, to us he signifies Thee!
Praised be my God for our sister the moon, and for the stars,
the which God has set clear and lovely in heaven.
Praised be my God for our brother the wind,
and for air and cloud, calms and all weather,
by the which thou upholdest in life all creatures.
Praised be my God for our sister water, who is
very serviceable unto us,
and humble, and precious, and clean.

Praised be my God for our brother fire, through whom
Thou givest us light in the darkness;
and he is bright, and pleasant,
and very mighty, and strong.
Praised be my God for our mother the earth, the which
doth sustain and keep us,
and bringeth forth divers fruits,
and flowers of many colours, and grass.
Praised be my God for all those who pardon one another
for Thy love's sake,
and who endure weakness and tribulation;
blessed are they who peaceably shall endure,
for Thou most highest, shalt give them a crown.
Praised be my God for our sister, the death of the body,
from whom no one escapeth.
Woe to those who die in mortal sin!
Blessed are they who are found walking by Thy most
holy will,
for the second death shall have no power to do
them harm.
Praise ye, and bless ye the Lord, and give thanks unto Thee,
and serve Thee with great humility.

—*St. Francis of Assisi, 1182–1226;* alt.

Born into a wealthy Italian family, Francis chose to follow the teachings of Jesus and serve the poor by living and working among them. His followers became known as Franciscans. This selection is called "The Canticle of the Creatures," translated by Matthew Arnold.

~

Well, Scholar, having taught you to paint your rod, and we having still a mile to Tottenham High Cross, I will, as we walk towards it in the cool shade of this sweet honeysuckle hedge, mention to you some of the thoughts and joys that have possessed my soul since we two met together.

And these thoughts shall be told you, that you also may join with me in thankfulness to "the Giver of every good and perfect gift" for our happiness. And that our present happiness may appear to be the greater, and we the more thankful for it, I will beg you to consider with me how many do, even at this very time, lie under the torment of the stone, the gout, and toothache; and this we are free from. And every misery that I miss is a new mercy: and therefore let us be thankful. There have been, since we met, others that have met disasters of broken limbs; some have been blasted, others thunderstrucken; and we have been freed from these: let us therefore rejoice and be thankful.

Nay, which is a far greater mercy, we are free from the unsupportable burthen of an accusing tormenting conscience; a misery that none can bear: and therefore let us praise God for good, preventing grace and say, Every misery that I miss is a new mercy. Nay, let me tell you, there be many that have forty times our estates, that would give the greatest part of it to be healthful and cheerful like us; who with the expense of a little money have eat, and drunk, and laughed, and angled, and sung, and slept securely; and rose next day, and cast away care, and sung, and laughed, and angled again; which are blessings the rich cannot purchase with all their money.

Let me tell you, Scholar, I have a rich neighbour that is always so busy that he has no leisure to laugh: the whole business of his life is to get money, and more money, that he may still get more and more money; he is still drudging on. . . .

Let us, therefore, be thankful for health and a competence and, above all, for a quiet conscience.

—*Izaak Walton, 1593–1683;* alt.

English writer and biographer Walton was by profession a London ironmonger and a devout Anglican. He is best remembered for the humorous dialogues in his writing entitled *The Compleat Angler,* from which this selection is taken.

~

With prayer goes gratitude. Thanksgiving is a real, interior, knowledge. With great reverence and loving fear, it turns us with all our powers to do whatever our [God] indicates. It brings joy and gratitude within. Sometimes its very abundance gives voice, "Good Lord, thank you and bless you!" And sometimes when the heart is dry and unfeeling or it may be because of the enemy's tempting—then reason and grace drive us to cry aloud . . . , recalling [God's] blessed passion and great goodness. And the strength of our [God's] Word comes to the soul, and fires the heart, and leads it by grace into its real business, enabling it to pray happily and to enjoy our [God] in truth. Thanksgiving is a blessed thing. . . .

—*Julian of Norwich, ca. 1332–1420;* alt.

A beloved English mystic, Julian was a cell-bound anchorite near a church in Norwich, where she experienced a series of divine visions. Her writings were entitled *Revelations of Divine Love,* from which this selection was taken. The translator was Clifton Wolters.

~

We thank you, God, we thank you,
    and declare your wonders.

Alleluia! Strength and might
be to the name of the Most High.
Zion is still God's city,
for it is God's dwelling place.
God still remembers the covenant with
our forebears, even in our generation.

God be praised! It goes well with us.
God is still our confidence.
God's protection, comfort and light
defend the city and palace.
God's wings keep the walls strong.
God dispenses blessing on us in every place.
Faithfulness, which kisses peace, must
forever meet righteousness.
Is there any people such as us,
to whom God is so near and gracious?
Remember us with your love,
Encircle us with your mercy.
Bless those who govern for us,
those who lead, protect and guide us;
bless those who are obedient.

Forget not in the future to show us
goodness with your hand.
So might our city and our land, which is
filled with your glory, praise you with
sacrifice and thanksgiving.
And let the people say: Amen.

—Anonymous librettist for Cantata 29
by Johann Sebastian Bach, 1685–1750

This cantata was composed in Leipzig in 1731 as Bach's contribution to the festivities surrounding the installation of a new city council and other leaders. This 1997 translation is by Mark Bangert.

~

It is in an especial manner our duty as a people, with devout reverence and affectionate gratitude, to acknowledge our many and great obligations to Almighty God, and to implore [God] to continue and confirm the blessings we experience.

Deeply penetrated with this sentiment, I, George Washington, President of the United States, do recommend to all religious societies and denominations, and to all persons whomsoever within the United States, to set apart and observe Thursday, the 19th day of February next, as a day of public thanksgiving and prayer, and on that day to meet together and render sincere and hearty thanks to the great God of nations for the manifold and signal mercies which distinguish our lot as a nation:

—particularly for the possession of constitutions of government which unite and, by their union, establish liberty with order; for the preservation of our peace, foreign and domestic; for the reasonable control which has been given to a spirit of disorder in the suppression of the late insurrection, and generally for the prosperous condition of our affairs, public and private,

—and at the same time humbly and fervently beseech the kind Author of these blessings graciously to prolong them to us;

—to imprint on our hearts a deep and solemn sense of our obligations to [God] for them; to teach us rightly to estimate their immense value;

—to preserve us from the arrogance of prosperity, and from hazarding the advantages we enjoy by delusive pursuits,

—to dispose us to merit the continuance of [God's] favors by not abusing them, by our gratitude for them, and by a corresponding conduct as citizens and [as a people] to render this country more and more a safe and propitious asylum for the unfortunate of other countries; to extend among us true and useful knowledge;

—to diffuse and establish habits of sobriety, order, and morality and piety, and finally to impart all the blessings we possess or ask for ourselves to the whole family of [humankind].

In testimony whereof, I have caused the seal of the United States of America to be affixed to these presents, and signed the same with my hand. Done at the city of Philadelphia the first day of January, 1795.

—*George Washington, 1732–1799;* alt.

Washington believed religion was the route to morality and that both were crucial to good government and prosperity.

~

If riches are a desirable possession in life,
    what is richer than wisdom, the active cause of all things?
And if understanding is effective,
    who more than she is fashioner of what exists?
And if anyone loves righteousness,
    her labors are virtues;
    for she teaches self-control and prudence,

justice and courage;
nothing in life is more profitable for mortals than these.

—*Wisdom of Solomon 8:5–7*

~

It is God who has made the night for you, that you may rest therein, and the day, as that which helps you to see. Verily God is full of grace and bounty to men, yet most men give no thanks.

It is God who has made for you the earth as a resting place, and the sky as a canopy, and has given you shape—and made your shapes beautiful—and has provided for you sustenance of things pure and good; such is God, your Lord. So glory to God, the Lord of the Worlds!

—*Qur'an 40.61, 64*

The Qur'an is described as the Divine Writ from Allah, sacred to all Muslims. Yusuf Ali is the translator of this piece.

~

Abraham caused God's name to be mentioned by all the travellers whom he entertained. For after they had eaten and drunk, and when they arose to bless Abraham, he said to them, "Is it of mine that you have eaten? Surely it is of what belongs to God that you have eaten. So praise and bless Him by whose word the world was created."

—*Talmud, Sota 10b*

The Talmud, a collection of teachings from Jewish tradition, is second in importance only to the twenty-two books of the Hebrew Bible. This selection is from *Rabbinic Anthology,* 1927.

~

O Creator, O God, I believe that Thou are Good, and Thou art pleas'd with the pleasure of Thy children.

Praised be Thy Name forever.

By Thy Power hast thou made the glorious Sun, with its attending worlds; from the energy of Thy mighty Will they first received their prodigious motion, and by Thy Wisdom hast Thou prescribed the wondrous laws by which they move.

Praised be Thy Name forever.

By Thy Wisdom hast thou formed all things, Thou hast created human beings, bestowing life and reason, and plac'd them in dignity superior to Thy other earthly Creatures.

Praised be Thy Name forever.

Thy Wisdom, Thy Power, and Thy Goodness are every where clearly seen; in the air and in the water, in the heavens and on the earth; Thou providest for the various winged fowl, and the innumerable inhabitants of the water; Thou givest cold and heat, rain and sunshine in their season, and to the fruits of the earth increase.

Praised be Thy Name forever.

I believe Thou hast given life to Thy creatures that they might live, and art not delighted with violent death and bloody sacrifices.

Praised be Thy Name forever.

Thou abhorrest in Thy creatures treachery and deceit, malice, revenge, Intemperance and every other hurtful Vice; but Thou art a Lover of justice and sincerity, of friendship, benevolence and every virtue. Thou art my Friend, . . . my Benefactor.

Praised be Thy Name, O God, forever.
Amen.

—*Benjamin Franklin, 1706–1790;* alt.

One of the writers of the U.S. Constitution in 1776, Franklin was a diplomat, inventor, and philosopher whose ideas enabled many groups to work together for the common good. This selection is from *The Papers of Benjamin Franklin.*

~

Sing praise to God, who has shaped and sustains all creation!
Sing praise, my soul, in profound and complete adoration!
Gladsome rejoice—organ, and trumpet, and voice—
Joining God's great congregation.

Praise God, our guardian, who lovingly offers correction,
Who, as on eagle's wings, saves us from sinful dejection.
Have you observed, how we are always preserved,
Through God, our parent's affection.

Sing praise to God, in thanksgiving for all your successes.
Merciful God ever loves to encourage and bless us.
Only conceive, what godly strength can achieve:
Strength that would touch and caress us.

Sing praise, my soul, the great name of your high God
commending.
All that has life and breath joins you, your notes sweetly
blending.
God is your light! Soul ever keep this in sight:
Amen, amen never ending.

—*Guaiacum Neander, 1650–1680*

A pastor of the Reformed Church in Düsseldorf, Germany, Neander wrote many hymn texts as well as the music for them. This selection was translated by Madeleine Forell Marshall in 1993.

~

The commonplace I sing;
How cheap is health! how cheap nobility!
Abstinence, no falsehood, no gluttony, lust;
The open air I sing, freedom, toleration,
(Take here the mainest lesson—less from books—
less from the schools),
The common day and night—the common earth
and waters,
Your farm—your work, trade, occupation,
The democratic wisdom underneath, like solid ground
for all.

—*Walt Whitman, 1819–1892*

Whitman celebrated the vastness of America and the resiliency of its people in his epic *Leaves of Grass* following years of wandering through the country. This selection from it is entitled "The Commonplace."

~

Chorus [While a Te Deum *is sung in Latin by a choir in the distance]:*
We praise Thee, O God, for Thy glory displayed in all
the creatures of the earth,
In the snow, in the rain, in the wind, in the storm; in all
of Thy creatures, both the hunters and the hunted.
For all things exist only as seen by Thee, only as known
by Thee, all things exist

Only in Thy light, and Thy glory is declared even in that
which denies Thee; the darkness declares the glory of
light.
Those who deny Thee could not deny, if Thou didst not
exist; and their denial is never complete, for if it were
so, they would not exist.
They affirm Thee in living; all things affirm Thee in living,
the bird in the air, both the hawk and the finch;
the beast on the earth, both the wolf and the lamb;
the worm in the soil and the worm in the belly.
Therefore man, whom Thou hast made to be conscious
of Thee, must consciously praise Thee, in thought and
in word and in deed.
Even with the hand to the broom, the back bent in laying
the fire, the knee bent in cleaning the hearth, we,
the scrubbers and sweepers of Canterbury,
The back bent under toil, the knee bent under sin,
the hands to the face under fear, the head bent
under grief,
Even in us the voices of seasons, the snuffle of winter,
the song of spring, the drone of summer, the voices
of beasts and of birds, praise Thee.
We thank Thee for Thy mercies of blood, for Thy
redemption by blood.
For the blood of Thy martyrs and saints shall enrich
the earth, shall create the holy places.
For wherever a saint has dwelt, wherever a martyr has
given his blood for the blood of Christ,
There is holy ground, and the sanctity shall not
depart from it;
Though armies trample over it, though sightseers come
with guide-books looking over it;

From where the western seas gnaw at the coast of Iona,
To the death in the desert, the prayer in forgotten
places by the broken imperial column,
From such ground springs that which forever renews
the earth
Though it is forever denied. Therefore, O God, we
thank Thee—
Who hast given such blessing to Canterbury.

—*T. S. Eliot, 1888–1964*

Thomas Stearns Eliot was an American-born British poet, dramatist, and critic. His most important drama was *Murder in the Cathedral,* 1935, from which this selection was taken. It is the story of the murder of the archbishop of Canterbury in the reign of Henry II.

~

Blessed are you, O God,
Creator of the universe,
who have made all things good
and given the earth for us to cultivate.
Grant that we may always use created things gratefully
and share your gifts with those in need.

—*Elizabeth Barrett Browning, 1806–1861*

Considered the greatest English woman poet, Elizabeth Browning is known for *Sonnets from the Portuguese,* 1850. This work is entitled "Earth's Crammed with Heaven."

~

It is He who sends down to you out of heaven water of which you may drink, and by which [grown] trees, for you to pasture your herds, and thereby He brings forth for you crops, and olives, and palms, and vines, and all manner of fruit. Surely in that is a sign for a people who reflect.

And He subjected for you the night and day, and the sun and moon; and the stars are subjected by His command. Surely in that are signs for a people who understand.

And He has multiplied for you in the earth things of diverse hues. Surely in that is a sign for a people who remember.

It is He who subjected for you the sea, that you may eat of it fresh flesh, and bring forth out of it ornaments for you to wear; and you may see the ships cleaving through it; that you may seek of His bounty, and so haply you will be thankful. . . .

If you count God's blessing, you can never number it; surely God is All-forgiving, All-compassionate.

—*Qur'an 16.10–18*

This selection is from *The Koran Interpreted,* Arthur J. Arberry, translator.

~

Now thank we all our God with heart and hands and voices,
Who wondrous things has done, in whom this world
 rejoices.
Who, from our parents' arms, has blessed us on our way
With countless gifts of love, and still is ours today.

O may this bounteous God through all our life be near us,
With ever joyful hearts and blessed peace to cheer us,
And keep us still in grace, and guide us when perplexed,
And free us from all ills in this world and the next.

All praise and thanks to God our Maker now be given,
To Christ, and Spirit, too, our help in highest heaven,
The one eternal God, whom earth and heaven adore,
For thus it was, is now, and shall be evermore.

—*Martin Rinkart, 1586–1649*

Pastor and musician Martin Rinkart served his parishioners in the east German town of Eisleben through the horrors of the Thirty Years' War. This famous hymn was first translated into English by Catherine Winkworth, 1829–1878, *alt.*

~

Most high and mighty Ruler of the universe,
by whom our Nation hath been established
in freedom and preserved in union;
We praise Thee for Thy favor shown unto our [forebears], and
Thy faithfulness continued unto their children:
for the rich land given us for an inheritance, and
the great power entrusted to the people:
for the fidelity of [those] set in authority, and
the peace maintained by righteous laws:
for protection against our enemies, and
deliverance from inward strife:
for an honorable place among the nations, and
the promise of increasing strength.
[God], Thou hast not dealt so with any people:
Keep Thou the Commonwealth beneath Thy care, and
guide the State according to Thy will: and
Thine shall be the glory and the praise and the thanksgiving,
from generation to generation.

—*From* The Book of Common Worship; alt.

This selection is from *A Book of Family Worship,* first published by the Presbyterian Board of Publications in 1916. The prayer is credited to an early edition of *The Book of Common Worship.*

~

In every highly developed religion the appreciation of moral obligation and duty, ranking as a claim of the deity upon [humankind], has been developed side by side with the religious feeling itself. Nonetheless a profoundly humble and heartfelt recognition of "the holy" may occur in particular experiences without being always or definitely charged or infused with the sense of moral demands. The "holy" will then be recognized as that which commands our respect, as that whose real value is to be acknowledged inwardly.

It is not that the awe of holiness is itself simply "fear" in face of what is absolutely overpowering, before which there is no alternative to blind, awestruck obedience. *"Tu solus sanctus"* is rather a paean of *praise,* which, so far from being merely a faltering confession of the divine supremacy, recognizes and extols a value, precious beyond all conceiving.

The object of such praise is not simply absolute might, making its claims and compelling their fulfillment, but a might that has at the same time the supremest right to make the highest claim to service, and receives praise because it is in an absolute sense worthy to be praised. "Thou art worthy to receive praise and honour and power" (Rev. 4:11).

—*Rudolf Otto, 1869–1937;* alt.

German theologian Otto's popular work, from which this excerpt is taken, is entitled *The Idea of the Holy,* first published in 1917 and translated into English in 1923 by John Harvey.

~

Whenever I felt the beauty of the world in song or story, in the material universe around me, or glimpsed it in human love, I wanted to cry out with joy. The Psalms were an outlet for this enthusiasm of joy or grief—and I suppose my writing was also an outlet. After all, one must communicate ideas.

I always felt the common unity of our humanity; the longing of the human heart is for this communion. If only I could sing, I thought, I would shout before the Lord, and call upon the world to shout with me, "All ye works of the Lord, bless ye the Lord, . . . forever."

—Dorothy Day, 1897–1980

A co-founder of the Catholic Worker Movement, Day called for a "permanent revolution" to redress social wrongs. This selection is from Day's autobiography, *The Long Loneliness.*

~

I taste a liquor never brewed,
From tankards scooped in pearl;
Not all the vats upon the Rhine
Yield such an alcohol!

Inebriate of air am I,
And debauchee of dew,
Reeling, through endless summer days,
From inns of molten blue.

When landlords turn the drunken bee
Out of the foxglove's door,
When butterflies renounce their drams,
I shall but drink the more!

Till seraphs swing their snowy hats,
And saints to windows run,
To see the little tippler
Leaning against the sun!

—*Emily Dickinson, 1830–1886*

American poet Dickinson spent nearly all of her life in the same house and yard in Amherst, Massachusetts. Only five of her hundreds of enigmatic and beautiful poems were published before her death.

~

The love wé feel for the splendour of the heavens, the plains, the sea and the mountains, for the silence of nature which is borne in upon us by its thousands of tiny sounds, for the breath of the winds, or the warmth of the sun, this love of which every human being has at least an inkling, is an incomplete, painful love, because it is felt for things which are incapable of responding, that is to say for matter.

[We] want to turn this same love towards a being who is like ourselves and capable of answering to our love, of saying yes, of surrendering. When the feeling for beauty happens to be associated with the sight of some human being, the transference of love is made possible, at any rate in an illusory manner. But it is all the beauty of the world, it is universal beauty, for which we yearn. . . .

The longing to love the beauty of the world in a human being is essentially the longing for the Incarnation. It is mistaken if it thinks it is anything else. The Incarnation alone can satisfy it. . . .

Beauty is eternity here below.

—*Simone Weil, 1909–1942;* alt.

Born in Paris, Weil showed a precocious talent for literature and science by the age of six and was recognized as a philosophical genius in advanced studies. This selection is from her book *Waiting for God,* 1951, translated by Emma Craufurd.

~

i thank You God for most this amazing
day:for the leaping greenly spirits of trees
and a blue true dream of sky;and for everything
which is natural which is infinite which is yes

(i who have died am alive again today,
and this is the sun's birthday;this is the birth
day of life and of love and wings;and of the gay
great happening illimitably earth)

how should tasting touching hearing seeing
breathing any—lifted from the no
of all nothing—human merely being
doubt unimaginable You?

(now the ears of my ears awake and
now the eyes of my eyes are opened)

—E. E. Cummings, 1894–1962

Novelist and poet Cummings enjoyed annoying critics with the eccentric punctuation and spacing in his poetic writings. Born in Cambridge, Massachusetts, he first came to attention in the poetry magazine *The Dial.*

~

O Light Invisible, we praise Thee!
Too bright for mortal vision.

O Greater Light, we praise Thee for the less;
The eastern light our spires touch at morning,
The light that slants upon our western doors at evening,
The twilight over stagnant pools at batflight,
Moon light and star light, owl and moth light,
Glow-worm glowlight on a grassblade.
O Light Invisible, we worship thee!

We thank Thee for the lights that we have kindled,
The light of altar and of sanctuary;
Small lights of those who meditate at midnight
And lights directed through the coloured panes of windows
And light reflected from the polished stone,
The gilded carven wood, the coloured fresco.
Our gaze is submarine, our eyes look upward
And see the light that fractures through unquiet water.
We see the light but see not whence it comes.
O Light Invisible, we glorify Thee!

In our rhythm of earthly life we tire of light. We are glad when the day ends, when the play ends; and ecstasy is too much pain.
We are children quickly tired: children who are up in the night and fall asleep as the rocket is fired; and the day is long for work or play.
We tire of distraction or concentration, we sleep and are glad to sleep,
Controlled by the rhythm of blood and the day and the night and the seasons.
And we must extinguish the candle, put out the light and relight it;
Forever must quench, forever relight the flame.

Therefore we thank Thee for our little light, that is
  dappled with shadow.
We thank Thee who has moved us to building, to finding,
  to forming at the ends of our fingers and beams
    of our eyes.
And when we have built an altar to the Invisible Light,
  we may set thereon the little lights for which our
    bodily vision is made.
And we thank Thee that darkness reminds us of light.
O Light Invisible, we give Thee thanks for Thy great glory!

—*T. S. Eliot, 1888–1964*

Born in St. Louis, Missouri, Eliot studied at Harvard, Paris, and Oxford before marrying and settling in England, where he became a citizen in 1927. His writings won the Nobel Prize in literature in 1948. This selection is from his play *The Rock*.

~

Immortal, invisible, God only wise,
In light inaccessible hid from our eyes,
Most blessed, most glorious, the Ancient of Days,
Almighty, victorious, thy great name we praise.

Unresting, unhasting, and silent as light,
Nor wanting, nor wasting, thou rulest in might,
Thy justice like mountains high soaring above
Thy clouds, which are fountains of goodness and love.

To all, life thou givest to both great and small;
In all life thou livest, the true life of all;
We blossom and flourish as leaves on the tree,
And wither and perish, but naught changeth thee.

Thou reignest in glory; thou dwellest in light,
Thine angels adore thee, all veiling their sight;
All laud we would render; O help us to see
'Tis only the splendor of light hideth thee.

—*Walter Chalmers Smith, 1824–1908*

Smith was a minister of the Free Church of Scotland and author of several volumes of poetry. This work was first published in Smith's 1867 hymnal, *Hymns of Christ and the Christian Life.*

~

We thank you, O God, for the saints of all ages;
For those who in times of darkness
  kept the lamp of faith burning;
For the great souls who saw visions of
  larger truth and dared to declare it;
For the multitude of quiet and gracious souls
  whose presence has purified and sanctified the world;
And for those known and loved by us,
  who have passed from this earthly fellowship
  into the fuller light of life with you.
Amen.

—*Anonymous*

~

Not to serve the foolish, but to serve the wise,
To honour those worthy of honour—this is the
  highest blessing.

Much insight and education, self-control and pleasant
  speech,

And whatever word be well-spoken—this is the
highest blessing.

Service to mother and father, the company of wife
and child,
And peaceful pursuits—this is the highest blessing.

Almsgiving and righteousness, the company of kinsfolk,
Blameless works—this is the highest blessing.

To dwell in a pleasant land, with right desire in the heart,
To bear remembrance of good deeds—this is the
highest blessing.

Reverence and humility, cheerfulness and gratitude,
listening in due season to the Dhamma—this is the
highest blessing.

Self-control and virtue, vision of the Noble Truths,
And winning to Nirvana—this is the highest blessing.

Beneath the stroke of life's changes, the mind that does
not shake
But abides without grief or passion—this is the highest
blessing.

On every side invincible are they who do thus,
They come to salvation—theirs is the highest blessing.

—*From the Sutta Nipāta, ca. 100* B.C.E.

On linguistic grounds, the Sutta Nipāta of collected discourses is believed to contain the oldest Buddhist writings that include the concept of equality in contrast to the hierarchies of traditional Hinduism.

~

The trees are getting bare, but still it stays warm. Coming down at night from the city, the warm, sweet smell of the good earth enwraps one like a garment. There is the smell of rotting applies; or alfalfa in the barn; burning leaves; of wood fires in the house; of pickled green tomatoes and baked beans.

Now there is a warm feeling of contentment about the farm these days—the first summer is over, many people have been cared for here, already. From day to day we did not know where the next money to pay bills was coming from, but trusting to our cooperators, our readers throughout the country, we went on with the work. Now all our bills are paid and there is a renewed feeling of courage on the part of all those who are doing the work, a sense of confidence that the work is progressing.

This month of thanksgiving will indeed be one of gratitude to God. For health, for work to do, for the opportunities . . . given us of service; we are deeply grateful, and it is a feeling that makes the heart swell with joy.

During the summer when things were going especially hard in more ways than one, I grimly modified grace before meals: "We give Thee thanks, O Lord, for these Thy gifts, and for all our tribulations, from Thy bounty, through Christ our Lord, Amen." One could know of certain knowledge that tribulations were matters of thanksgiving; that we were indeed privileged to share in the sufferings of Our Lord. So in this month of thanksgiving, we can be thankful for the trials of the past, the blessings of the present, and be heartily ready at the same time to embrace with joy any troubles the future may bring us.

—*Dorothy Day, 1897–1980*

Catholic social activist and pacifist, journalist Day wrote monthly columns for the newspaper *The Catholic Worker,* from which this excerpt was taken (November 1936).

~

Who has measured the waters in the hollow of his hand
    and marked off the heavens with a span,
    enclosed the dust of the earth in a measure
    and weighed the mountains in scales
    and the hills in a balance?
Who has directed the spirit of the Lord,
    or as his counselor has instructed him?
Whom did he consult for his enlightenment,
    and who taught him the path of justice?

All the nations are as nothing before him,
    they are accounted by him as less than nothing and
    emptiness.

Have you not known? Have you not heard? The Lord is
  the everlasting God,
    the Creator of the ends of the earth.
He does not faint or grow weary,
    his understanding is unsearchable.
He gives power to the faint,
    and strengthens the powerless.
Even youths will faint and be weary,
    and the young will fall exhausted;
    but those who wait for the Lord shall renew
        their strength,
    they shall mount up with wings like eagles,

they shall run and not be weary,
they shall walk and not faint.

—Isaiah 40:12–14a, 17, 28–31

~

O Eternal God, though Thou art not such as I can see with my eyes or touch with my hands, yet grant me this day a clear conviction of Thy reality and power. Let me not go forth to my work believing only in the world of sense and time, but give me grace to understand that the world I cannot see or touch is the most real world of all. My life today will be lived in time, but eternal issues will be concerned in it. The needs of my body will be clamant, but it is for the needs of my soul that I must care most. My business will be with things material, but behind them let me be aware of things spiritual. Let me keep steadily in mind that the things that matter are not money or possessions, not houses or lands, not bodily comfort or bodily pleasure; but truth and honour and meekness and helpfulness and a pure love of Thyself.

For the power Thou hast given me to lay hold
of things unseen;
For the strong sense I have that this is not my home;
For my restless heart which nothing finite can satisfy;
I give Thee thanks, O God.
For the invasion of my soul by Thy Holy Spirit;
For all human love and goodness that speak to me
of Thee;
For the fullness of Thy glory outpoured in Jesus Christ.

I, a pilgrim of eternity, stand before Thee, O eternal One. Let me not seek to deaden or destroy the desire for Thee that disturbs my heart. Let me rather yield myself to its constraint and go where it leads me. Make me wise to see all things today under the form of eternity, and make me brave to face all the changes in my life which such a vision may entail: through the grace of Christ my Saviour. Amen.

—*John Baillie, 1886–1960*

Scottish theologian and church leader John Baillie is the author of one of the most popular devotional books of the '40s and '50s, *A Diary of Private Prayer,* from which this selection was taken.

~

This is the day which the Lord hath made,
Shining like Eden absolved of sin,
Three parts glitter to one part shade:
Let us be glad and rejoice therein.

Everything's scoured brighter than metal.
Everything sparkles as pure as glass—
The leaf on the poplar, the zinnia's petal,
The wing of the bird, and the blade of grass.

All, all is luster. The glossy harbor
Dazzles the gulls that, gleaming, fly.
Glimmers the wasp on the grape in the arbor.
Glisten the clouds in the polished sky.

Tonight—tomorrow—the leaf will fade,
The waters tarnish, the dark begin.
But this is the day which the Lord hath made:
Let us be glad and rejoice therein.

—*Phyllis McGinley, 1905–1978*

McGinley won the Pulitzer Prize in poetry in 1961 with her book *Times Three.* This selection is entitled "Sunday Psalm."

~

O God, to Thee we owe our life and the joys that weave themselves into it; to Thee we owe our loved ones, with all the delight of their companionship. Thy goodness has clothed the world in glorious raiment, and given us the power to feel its splendour. To Thee we owe the pleasures of the mind, the joy of books and the ennobling influence of art. And to Thee we owe, above all, the instinctive sense of Thy presence, the stir of the spirit which bids us seek after Thee, the aspirations which lift us above the lesser concerns of life into an air ampler and purer.

—*From* Liberal Jewish Prayer Book, *19th century*

~

To what purpose, April, do you return again?
Beauty is not enough.
You can no longer quiet me with the redness
Of little leaves opening stickily.
I know what I know.
The sun is hot on my neck as I observe
The spikes of the crocus.
The smell of the earth is good.
It is apparent that there is no death.
But what does that signify?
Not only underground are the brains of men
Eaten by maggots.
Life in itself

Is nothing,
An empty cup, a flight of uncarpeted stairs.
It is not enough that yearly, down this hill,
April
Comes like an idiot, babbling and strewing flowers.

—*Edna St. Vincent Millay, 1892–1950*

A dramatist, poet, librettist, and short-story writer, Millay was a prodigy whose first long poem, "Renascence," was published when she was barely 19. This selection is entitled "April."

~

Glory be to God for dappled things—
    For skies of purple-color as a brindled cow;
        For rose-moles all in stipple upon trout that swim;
Fresh-firecoal chestnut-falls; finches' wings;
    Landscape plotted and pieced—fold, fallow, and plough;
        And all trades, their gear and tackle and trim.
All things counter, original, spare, strange;
    Whatever is fickle, freckled (who knows how?)
        With swift, slow; sweet, soul; adazzle, dim;
He fathers-forth whose beauty is past change:
            Praise him.

—*Gerard Manley Hopkins, 1844–1889*

When Hopkins became a Jesuit in 1868, he burned most of his poems, saving only a remnant. None were published during his lifetime, but the "remnant" has made him one of the major metaphysical poets of the nineteenth century.

~

Lord, behold our family here assembled.
We thank you for this place in which we dwell,
    for the love that unites us,
    for the peace accorded us this day,
    for the hope with which we expect the morrow;
    for the health, the work, the food and the bright skies
        that make our lives delightful;
    for our friends in all parts of the earth.
Give us courage and gaiety and the quiet mind,
Spare us to our friends, soften us to our enemies.
Bless us, if it may be, in all our innocent endeavours;
    if it may not, give us the strength to endure that
      which is to come
    that we may be brave in peril, constant in tribulation,
    temperate in wrath and in all changes of fortune
    and down to the gates of death,
    loyal and loving, one to another.
As the clay to the potter
    as the windmill to the wind
    as children of their sire,
    we beseech of you this help and mercy
    for Christ's sake.

—*Robert Louis Stevenson, 1850–1894*

A Scottish writer, best known for his novel *Treasure Island,* Stevenson also wrote many prayers.

~

How good it is to center down!
To sit quietly and see one's self pass by!
The streets of our minds seethe with endless traffic;

Our spirits resound with clashings, with noisy silences,
While something deep within hungers and thirsts for
the still moment and the resting lull.
With full intensity we seek, ere the quiet passes,
a fresh sense of order in our living;
A direction, a strong sure purpose that will structure
our confusion and bring meaning in our chaos.
We look at ourselves in this waiting moment—
the kinds of people we are.
The questions persist: what are we doing with our lives?—
what are the motives that order our days?
What is the end of our doings? Where are we trying to go?
Where do we put the emphasis and where are our
values focused?
For what end do we make sacrifices? Where is my treasure
and what do I love most in life?
What do I hate most in life and to what am I true?
Over and over the questions beat in upon the
waiting moment.
As we listen, floating up through all the jangling echoes
of our turbulence, there is a sound of another kind—
A deeper note which only the stillness of the heart
makes clear.
It moves directly to the core of our being. Our questions
are answered.
Our spirits refreshed, and we move back into the traffic
of our daily round.
With the peace of the Eternal in our step.
How good it is to center down!

—*Howard Thurman, 1899–1981*

Baptist minister Thurman first served a church in Oberlin, Ohio, and later became a professor of religion at various colleges. He wrote many books of devotions and social commentary. This selection is from *Meditations of the Heart,* 1953.

~

Gratitude is one of the most visible characteristics of the poor I have come to know. I am always surrounded by words of thanks: "thanks for your visit, your blessing, your sermon, your prayer, your gifts, your presence with us." Even the smallest and most necessary goods are a reason for gratitude. This all-pervading gratitude is the basis for celebration. Not only are the poor grateful for life, but they also celebrate life constantly. A visit, a reunion, a simple meeting are always like little celebrations. . . . All of life is a gift, a gift to be celebrated, a gift to be shared.

—*Henri Nouwen, 1932–1996*

Father Nouwen was born in Holland, where he became a Roman Catholic priest in 1957. He taught at the University of Notre Dame and Yale University. This selection is from *¡Gracias!,* his journal from Latin America.

~

All, absolutely all,
by your grace
speaks to me of You.

When I write
I ask
in your hands to be

the blank sheet of paper
where You can write what You please.

When I skim through a book
I feel acutely anxious
that such a lot of words should not go fruitless
and that no one should write
without some happy message for the world.

Every step I take
reminds me
that, wherever I am going
I am always on the march to eternity.

The din of human life,
the dry leaves eddying on the ground,
the passing cars,
shop-windows full of goods,
the policeman on point-duty,
the milk-float,
the poor man begging,
the staircase and the lift,
the railway lines, the furrows of the sea,
the pedigree dog and the ownerless dog,
the pregnant woman,
the paper-boy,
the man who sweeps the streets,
the church, the school,
the office and the factory,
streets being widened,
hills being laid low,
the outward and the homeward road,
the key I use to open my front door;

whether sleeping or waking—
all, all, all
makes me think of You.

What can I give to the Lord
for all He has given to me?

—*Dom Helder Camara*

Archbishop of Olinda and Recife in northeast Brazil, the poorest and least developed region of the country, Camara writes his poetry during nightly vigils. In 1970, he received the international Martin Luther King, Jr. Award. This selection is from *A Thousand Reasons for Living,* 1981.

~

Much has changed for America in the two centuries since that first Thanksgiving proclamation. Generations of hard-working men and women have cultivated our soil and worked the land, and today America's bounty helps feed the world.

The promise of freedom that sustained our founders through the hardships of the Revolution and the first challenging days of nationhood has become a reality for millions of immigrants who left their homelands for a new life on these shores. And the light of that freedom now shines brightly in many nations that once lived in the shadows of tyranny and oppression.

But across the years, we still share an unbroken bond with the men and women who first proclaimed Thanksgiving in our land.

Americans today still cherish the fresh air of freedom, in which we can raise our families and worship God as we choose without fear of persecution. We still rejoice in this great land and in the civil and religious liberty it offers to all. And we still, and always, raise our voices in prayer to God, [giving thanks] in humility for the countless blessings . . . bestowed on our nation and our people.

Let us now, this Thanksgiving Day, reawaken ourselves and our neighbors and our communities to the genius of our founders in daring to build the world's first constitutional democracy on the foundation of trust and thanks to God. Out of our right and proper rejoicing on Thanksgiving Day, let us give our own thanks to God and reaffirm our love of family, neighbor, and community.

Each of us can be an instrument of blessing to those we touch this Thanksgiving Day—and every day of the year.

—*William J. Clinton;* alt.

This excerpt is from President Clinton's 1996 Thanksgiving Day proclamation.

~

The earth is God's and all that is in it,
    the world, and those who live in it;
    for God has founded it on the seas,
    and established it on the rivers.
Who shall ascend the hill of God?
And who shall stand in God's holy place?
Those who have clean hands and pure hearts,
    who do not lift up their souls to what is false,
    and do not swear deceitfully.
They will receive blessing from God,
    and vindication from the God of their salvation.

Such is the company of those who seek God,
who seek the face of the God of Jacob. *Selah*

—*Psalm 24:1–6*

~

Almighty God, giver of all good things:
We thank you for the natural majesty and beauty of this land.
They restore us, though we often destroy them.
Heal us.
We thank you for the great resources of this nation.
They make us rich, though we often exploit them.
Forgive us.
We thank you for the men and women who have made this country strong.
They are models for us, though we often fall short of them.
Inspire us.
We thank you for the torch of liberty which has been lit in this land.
It has drawn people from every nation, though we have often hidden from its light.
Enlighten us.
We thank you for the faith we have inherited in all its rich variety.
It sustains our life, though we have been faithless again and again.
Renew us.

Help us, O Lord, to finish the good work here begun. Strengthen our efforts to blot out ignorance and prejudice, and to abolish poverty and crime. And hasten the day when all our people, with many voices in one united chorus, will glorify your holy Name.
Amen.

—*The Book of Common Prayer*

This selection is entitled "Thanksgiving for National Life."

~

Wondrous, wondrous, wondrous, wondrous, wondrous is thy Name,
False, false, false, false is worldly pride.
Priceless are thy devotees, beauteous their countenance.
Without thy Name, the world is but ashes.
Wondrous is thy power and praiseworthy thy steps.
Priceless is thy praise, O True King.
Thou art the only refuge of thy supportless creatures.
Ever dwell on God, the pride of the poor.
The lord Himself is merciful unto Nanak.
May I not forget God, Who is my mind, soul, and Life.

—*Sikh* Shabad: *Hymn of Praise*

Shabads are the holy hymns of Sikhism. Sikhism teaches meditation on God's name, earning an honest living, sharing good fortune with the needy, and serving God's creation as essential tenets.

~

My faith, which has anchored my life, begins with a joyful gratitude that there is a God who created the universe and then, because He continued to care for what He created, gave us laws and values to order and improve our lives.

God also gave us a purpose and a destiny—to do justice and to protect, indeed to perfect, the human community and natural environment. In trying to live according to these principles, I am helped by daily prayer and religious rituals such as observance of the Sabbath—a time to stop and appreciate all that God has given us. I also find strength and humility in being linked to something so much larger and longer-lasting than myself.

To me, being Jewish also means the joy of being part of a unique ethnic culture and reveling in its history and humor, its language and literature, its music and moods, its festivals and foods.

Being Jewish in America also means feeling a special love for this country, which has provided such unprecedented freedom and opportunity to the millions who have come and lived here. My parents raised me to believe that I did not have to mute my religious faith or ethnic identity to be a good American, that, on the contrary, America invites all its people to be what they are and believe what they wish. In truth, it is from our individual diversity and shared faith in God that we Americans draw our greatest strength and hope.

—*Joseph I. Lieberman*

A U.S. senator from Connecticut, Lieberman wrote this essay in 1992 for the American Jewish Committee.

~

God of the ages, who with sure command
brought forth in beauty all the starry band
of shining worlds in splendor through the skies,
our grateful songs before your throne arise.

Your purpose, just, envisions mortals free;
God, set our path toward human liberty.
Still be our ruler, guardian, guide, and stay—
your Word our law, your paths our chosen way.

From war's alarms, from deadly pestilence,
with steadfast care be ever our defense;
Your love and faith within our hearts increase;
your bounteous goodness nourish us in peace.

Refresh your people on life's toilsome way;
lead us from night to neverending day;
With truth and love guide us through error's maze,
and we shall give you glory, laud, and praise.

—*Daniel Crane Roberts, 1841–1907;* alt.

As the 35-year-old rector of a small Episcopal church in Vermont, Roberts decided that America should have a new national hymn for its hundredth birthday. His parishioners first sang this on July 4, 1876.

~

Today, I make my Sacrament of Thanksgiving.
I begin with the simple things of my days:
    Fresh air to breathe,
    Cool water to drink,
    The taste of food,
    The protection of houses and clothes,
    The comforts of home.
For all these I make an act of Thanksgiving this day!

I bring to mind all the warmth of humankind that I have known:

My mother's arms,
The strength of my father,
The playmates of my childhood,
The wonderful stories brought to me from the lives of many who talked of days gone by when fairies and giants and all kinds of magic held sway,
The tears I have shed, the tears I have seen,
The excitement of laughter and the twinkle in the eye with its reminder that life is good.
For all these I make an act of Thanksgiving this day.

I finger one by one the messages of hope that awaited me at the crossroads:
The smile of approval from those who held in their hands the reins of my security;
The tightening of the grip in a single handshake when I feared the step before me in the darkness;
The whisper in my heart when the temptation was fiercest and the claims of appetite were not to be denied;
The crucial word said, the simple sentence from an open page when my decision hung in the balance.
For all these I make an act of Thanksgiving this day.

I pass before me the mainsprings of my heritage:
The fruits of the labors of countless generations who lived before me, without whom my own life would have no meaning;
The seers who saw visions and dreamed dreams;
The prophets who sensed a truth greater than the mind could grasp, and whose words could only find fulfillment in the years which they would never see;

The workers whose sweat has watered the trees, the leaves
of which are for the healing of the nations;
The pilgrims who set their sails for lands beyond all
horizons, whose courage made paths into
new worlds and far-off places;
The saviors whose blood was shed with a
recklessness that only a dream could inspire
and God could command.
For all these I make an act of Thanksgiving this day.

I linger over the meaning of my own life and the
commitment to which I give the loyalty of my heart
and mind:
The little purposes in which I have shared with my loves,
my desires, my gifts;
The restlessness which bottoms all I do with its stark insistence that I have never done my best, I have never
reached for the highest;
The big hope that never quite deserts me, that I and my
kind will study war no more, that love and tenderness
and all the inner graces of Almighty affection will
cover the life of the children of God as the waters
cover the sea.

All these and more than mind can think and heart can feel,
I make as my sacrament of Thanksgiving to Thee,
Our Father, in humbleness of mind and simplicity of heart.

—*Howard Thurman, 1899–1981*

This selection from Thurman's *Meditations of the Heart* reflects his lifelong devotional stance toward life. Thurman's works continue to be spiritual classics.

~

YANG: . . .When we strike a nucleus with a fast projectile, it breaks up into many pieces. If physics was interested simply in cataloging these pieces, it would be a useless field and would not attract our interest. Instead, what we find is the patterns of these very complicated phenomena, and these patterns generate laws which are written in the form of equations, and these equations amazingly agree with experiment. So we know that nature has an order, and this order we can aspire to comprehend because past experience has told us that when we did more research, we comprehended large new areas of physics, and they are beautiful, and they are powerful.

MOYERS: Beautiful?

YANG: Yes, because if you can reduce many, many complicated phenomena to a few equations, that's a great beauty.

What is poetry? Poetry is a condensation of thought. You write in a few lines a very complicated thought. And when you do this, it becomes very beautiful poetry. It becomes powerful poetry. The equations we seek are the poetry of nature.

MOYERS: You make me think that maybe the poets anticipated you physicists. It was Blake, after all, who talked about seeing the universe in a grain of sand.

YANG: Yes, yes, that was a beautiful poem! We do have that feeling when we are confronted with something which we know is concentrated structure. When we reflect that this is a secret of nature, there is oftentimes a deep feeling of awe. It's as if we are seeing something that we shouldn't see.

MOYERS: Shouldn't see? Forbidden territory?

YANG: Yes, because it has a certain aura of sacredness, of power. When you are confronted with that, undoubtedly you have a feeling that this shouldn't have been seen by [mortals]. I oftentimes describe that as the deeper religious feeling. Of course, this brings us to the question which nobody knows how to answer: Why is nature that way? Why is it possible for these powerful manifestations of forces to be trapped in a very simple, beautiful formula? This has been a question which many people have discussed, but there's no answer. But the fact is, it is possible to do that, and it is possible to do more, and that's, of course, what entices us on. We want to build these machines not because we want to spend four billion dollars of public money, and not because we enjoy cataloging all the particles. Those are not the reasons at all. It is because there is something intrinsically good, intrinsically mysterious, and eventually, presumably, intrinsically powerful about this—and also extremely beautiful.

—*Chen Ning Yang and Bill Moyers;* alt.

This selection is from an interview appearing in *Bill Moyers: A World of Ideas—Conversations with Thoughtful Men and Women about American Life Today and the Ideas Shaping Our Future,* based on Moyer's public television program. Chen Ning Yang, a professor of physics (SUNY), was co-recipient of the Nobel Prize for physics in 1957.

~

If I think that belief in creation simply means finding God in my inner parts, enjoying a beautiful sunset, marveling over a hummingbird, pondering a child's birth, being thankful for blessings on Thanksgiving Day or admiring a sonata—all good things to do—nothing "humbling" or "terrifying" occurs. I am missing something—terror.

If I examine my limits, or recognize that the sunset signals not only the end of a day but the end of all things, terror threatens. If one sees only the beauty of nature or the wonder of childbirth and cannot anticipate the horror of what happens to children in a warring world, there is only illusion.

And more: Being thankful *for* is not the point of faith; being thankful *to* is. This demands humbling faith, not a warm Thanksgiving Day glow.

And admiring that sonata can easily lead one to be content with awe for human achievement without leading one to think back to its source.

A modern French treatment of *La Creation* by R. Guelluy has it right: "To believe in creation is to see Someone behind all things . . . to see the world as a gift."

—*Martin E. Marty*

Author of *The One and the Many: America's Struggle for the Common Good,* 1997, Marty is the religious leader most quoted in the media about matters of national interest. He is a historian, a pastor, and director of the scholarly Public Religion Project.

~

To know and to serve God, of course, is why we're here, a clear truth that, like the nose on your face, is near at hand and easily discernible but can make you dizzy if you try to focus on it hard. But a little faith will see you through.

What else will do *except* faith in such a cynical, corrupt

time? When the country goes temporarily to the dogs, cats must learn to be circumspect, walk on fences, sleep in trees, and have faith that all this woofing is not the last word.

—*Garrison Keillor*

A humorist from Minnesota, Keillor became known through his National Public Radio program *A Prairie Home Companion* and his book *Lake Wobegon Days,* 1985. This selection is from his book *We Are Still Married,* 1989.

~

Joyful, joyful we adore thee,
God of glory, Lord of love!
Hearts unfold like flow'rs before thee,
Praising thee, their sun above.
Melt the clouds of sin and sadness,
Drive the gloom of doubt away.
Giver of immortal gladness,
Fill us with the light of day.

All thy works with joy surround thee,
Earth and heav'n reflect thy rays,
Stars and angels sing around thee,
Center of unbroken praise,
Field and forest, vale and mountain,
Flow'ry meadow, flashing sea,
Changing bird, and flowing fountain
Call us to rejoice in thee.

Thou art giving and forgiving
Ever blessing, ever blest,
Wellspring of the joy of living,

Ocean-depth of happy rest!
Thou our Father, Christ our brother,
All who live in love are thine;
Teach us how to love each other,
Lift us to the joy divine!

—Henry van Dyke, 1852–1933

Van Dyke was a noted Presbyterian minister and church leader, Navy chaplain in World War I, U.S. ambassador to Holland and Luxembourg, and writer of devotional material. He insisted that his text for this hymn be sung to the music of "Hymn to Joy" from Beethoven's Ninth Symphony, a combination that has made it immortal.

~

Grant us peace, Thy most precious gift
O Thou eternal source of peace
Bless our country that it may be a stronghold of peace
May contentment reign within its borders
Bonds of friendship throughout the world
Plant virtue in every soul and love for Thy name
in every heart.

—Jewish Traditional

Sim Shalom is a traditional Jewish prayer song often used in interfaith settings.

Copyright Acknowledgments

"Prayer" by Robert H. Adams Jr. from *A Traveler's Prayer Book.* Copyright 1965 by The Upper Room, Nashville, Tennessee. Adapted, 1983, WCC Publications, World Council of Churches, Geneva, Switzerland. Used by permission.

Maya Angelou. From "Visions: Maya Angelou . . . " Reprinted with permission from *Mother Jones* magazine, © 1995, Foundation for National Progress.

Johann Sebastian Bach. Anonymous librettist for Cantata 29. Translated by Mark Bangert. Used by permission.

John Baillie. Reprinted with the permission of Scribner, a division of Simon & Schuster, from *A Diary of Private Prayer* by John Baillie. Copyright 1949 by Charles Scribner's Sons; copyright renewed © 1977 by Ian Fowler Baillie.

Excerpts of conversations with Mary Catherine Bateson and Chen Ning Yang. From *Bill Moyers: A World of Ideas* by Bill Moyers. Copyright © 1989 by Public Affairs Television, Inc. Used by permission of Doubleday, a division of Bantam Doubleday Dell Publishing Group, Inc.

Robert N. Bellah. Excerpt from "Living Out the Ecumenical Vision in America Today," 1992. Reprinted with permission of the author.

The Bible quotations are from: (1) the New Revised Standard Version (NRSV), copyrighted 1989 by the Division of Christian Education of the National Council of the Churches of Christ in the United States of America, and (2) *The New Testament and Psalms: An Inclusive Version,* an adaptation of the NRSV, copyrighted 1995 by Oxford University Press, Inc. These quotations are used by permission. All rights reserved.

Extracts from The Book of Common Prayer, the rights in which are vested in the Crown, are reproduced with permission of the Crown's Patentee, Cambridge University Press.

Dom Helder Camara. "All, Absolutely All." Reprinted from the English translation of *A Thousand Reasons for Living* by Dom Helder Camara, translated by Alan Neame, copyright © 1981 Darton, Longman and Todd. Used by permission of Augsburg Fortress.

Judy Chicago. "Merger" from *Prayers for All People,* chosen by Mary Ford-Grabowsky, Doubleday, 1995. © Judy Chicago, 1979. Used by permission.

Council for a Parliament of the World's Religions. Excerpt from "The Declaration of a Global Ethic." 1993. Reprinted with permission.

E. E. Cummings. "a man who had fallen among thieves," Copyright 1926, 1954, © 1991 by the Trustees for the E. E. Cummings Trust. Copyright © 1985 by George James Firmage, from *Complete Poems: 1904–1962* by E. E. Cummings, edited by George J. Firmage. Reprinted by permission of Liveright Publishing Corporation. "i thank You God for most this amazing," copyright 1950, © 1978, 1991 by the Trustees for the E. E. Cummings Trust. Copyright © 1979 by George James Firmage, from *Complete Poems: 1904–1962* by E. E. Cummings, edited by George J. Firmage. Reprinted by permission of Liveright Publishing Corporation.

Dorothy Day. Excerpts from a column written by Dorothy Day appearing in *The Catholic Worker:* "The trees are getting bare . . . " (November 1936) and "A Room for Christ" (December 1945). Used with permission.

"Day of Atonement" prayer. From *Forms of Prayer for Jewish Worship,* vol. 1, *Daily and Sabbath Prayer Book,* Reform Synagogues of Great Britain, London, 1977. Used by permission.

Diana L. Eck. From *Encountering God* by Diana L. Eck, © 1993 by Diana L. Eck. Reprinted by permission of Beacon Press, Boston.

Marian Wright Edelman. Prayer from *Guide My Feet* by Marian Wright Edelman, © 1995 by Marian Wright Edelman. Reprinted by permission of Beacon Press, Boston.

Robert L. Edwards. Words © 1961. Renewal 1989 by The Hymn Society. Used by permission of Hope Publishing Co., Carol Stream, IL 60188. All rights reserved.

T. S. Eliot. Excerpt from "Choruses from the Rock" in *Collected Poems 1909–1962* by T. S. Eliot, copyright 1936 by Harcourt Brace & Company, copyright © 1964, 1963 by T. S. Eliot, reprinted by permission of the publisher. Excerpts from *Murder in the Cathedral* by T. S. Eliot, copyright 1935 by Harcourt Brace & Company and renewed 1963 by T. S. Eliot, reprinted by permission of the publisher.

T. Simon Farisani. "Greed" from *Justice in My Tears* by Tshenuwani Simon Farisani. Copyright 1988. Trenton, N.J.: Africa World Press, Inc.

Ford Foundation. Excerpt from *The Common Good: Social Welfare and the American Future: Policy Recommendations of the Executive Panel.* Ford Foundation Project on Social Welfare and the American Future. Copyright 1980. Used with permission.

Lorraine Hansberry. Excerpt from *A Raisin in the Sun* by Lorraine Hansberry, Copyright © 1958 by Robert Nemiroff, as an unpublished work. Copyright © 1959, 1966, 1984 by Robert Nemiroff. Reprinted by permission of Random House, Inc.

Riffat Hassan. "Jihād Fī Sabīl Allah: A Muslim Woman's Faith Journey from Struggle to Struggle to Struggle," from *Women's and Men's Liberation: Testimonies of Spirit,* edited by Leonard Grob, Riffat Hassan, and Haim Gordon. Copyright 1991 by Leonard Grob, Riffat Hassan, and Haim Gordon. Reproduced with permission of Greenwood Publishing Group, Inc., Westport, Connecticut.

Langston Hughes. "Daybreak in Alabama" from *Selected Poems* by Langston Hughes, Copyright 1948 by Alfred A. Knopf, Inc., and renewed 1976 by the Executor of the Estate of Langston Hughes. Reprinted by permission of the publisher.

Interfaith Conference of Metropolitan Washington. Excerpt from "Statement on the Challenges Facing Us in the Aftermath of the Verdict in the Rodney King Trial," May 7, 1992. Reprinted with permission.

Martin Luther King Jr. Excerpt from "I Have a Dream" speech, Copyright 1963 by Martin Luther King, Jr.; copyright renewed 1991 by Coretta Scott King. Excerpt from "I've Been to the Mountaintop" speech, Copyright 1968 by the Estate of Martin Luther King, Jr. Reprinted by arrangement with The Heirs to the Estate of Martin Luther King, Jr., c/o Writers House, Inc., as agent for the proprietor.

Joseph Lieberman. "What Being Jewish Means to Me," excerpt from text of newspaper advertisement sponsored by American Jewish Committee. 1992. Used with permission.

Peter Marshall. "America Confesses," from *The Prayers of Peter Marshall* by Peter Marshall. Fleming H. Revell, a division of Baker Book House Company, Grand Rapids, Michigan. Copyright 1954. Used with permission.

Martin E. Marty. Excerpt from "Words for Today," *The Lutheran,* October 1992. Used with permission of the author.

Phyllis McGinley. "Sunday Psalm," from *Times Three* by Phyllis McGinley. Copyright 1932–1960 by Phyllis McGinley; Copyright 1938–42, 1944, 1945, 1958, 1959 by The Curtis Publishing Co. Used by permission of Viking Penguin, a division of Penguin Books USA Inc.

Edna St. Vincent Millay. "April," from *Collected Poems,* HarperCollins, Copyright 1921, 1948 by Edna St. Vincent Millay.

National Conference of Catholic Bishops. Excerpts from *Economic Justice for All,* © 1986 United States Catholic Conference (USCC), *Footnote 1:* Pastoral Constitution on the Church in the Modern World, 26; *Footnote 2:* Pope John Paul II, address at the General Assembly of the United Nations, October 2, 1979, Nos. 13 & 14; *Footnote 3:* See Pope Pius 12th, 1941 Pentecost Address in V. Yzermans, *The Major Addresses of Pope Pius 12th,* vol. 1, St. Paul: North Central, 1961, 32–33; and *Putting Children and Families First,* © 1991 USCC are used with permission.

Guaiacum Neander. "Sing Praise to God." Translation by Madeleine Forell Marshall, Copyright 1993. Used by permission.

Alan Paton. Excerpts from *Instrument of Thy Peace* by Alan Paton. Copyright © 1968, 1982 by the Seabury Press, Inc. Reprinted by permission of HarperCollins Publishers, Inc.

Eleanor Roosevelt. "My Day" reprinted by permission of United Feature Syndicate, Inc.

"God of Justice" from *The Sacramentary* (revised edition), © 1969, International Committee on English in the Liturgy, Inc. All rights reserved.

Dorothy Sayers. *The Man Born to Be King: A Play-Cycle on the Life of Our Lord and Saviour Jesus Christ,* Copyright 1943 Dorothy L. Sayers; Harper & Row Publishers, New York, Evanston, and London. Reprinted by permission of the Estate of Dorothy Sayers and the Watkins/Loomis Agency.

Dorothee Soelle. Reprinted by permission from *Theology for Skeptics* by Dorothee Soelle, translated by Joyce L. Irwin, Copyright © 1995 Augsburg Fortress.

Thích Nhât Hanh. "A Buddhist Litany for Peace." Reprinted with permission of Parallax Press, Berkeley, California.

Paul Tillich. Reproduced from *Theology of Peace* by Paul Tillich, edited and introduced by Ronald H. Stone. © 1990 Westminster/John Knox Press. Used by permission of Westminster John Knox Press.

Howard Thurman. Excerpts from *Meditations of the Heart* by Howard Thurman. © 1981 Howard Thurman. Reprinted by permission of the Howard Thurman Educational Trust.

Evelyn Underhill. Excerpts from *The Spiritual Life* by Evelyn Underhill. Copyright 1951 HarperCollins Publishers. Used with permission.

United Nations Documents. From UN Publication Board. Used by permission.

Henry van Dyke. "Joyful, Joyful We Adore Thee." Reprinted with the permission of Scribner, a division of Simon & Schuster, from *The Poems of Henry van Dyke* (New York: Charles Scribner's Sons, 1920). Copyright © 1911, 1920.

Nancy Lynne Westfield. "I Must Tell Jesus" prayer. Reprinted with permission of the author.

Miriam Therese Winter. "It would have been enough . . . " from *WomanWisdom,* Copyright 1991 Medical Mission Sisters. Used with permission of the Crossroad Publishing Company.

Index of Authors and Sources

About the Author

A. Jean Lesher, a writer and book developer, most recently was director of copyrights and permissions for the American Bar Association. She has also been a book editor for major educational publishers.

Praise for *Prayers for the Common Good*

"*Prayers for the Common Good* is a reminder that prayer is not really a 'religious' act, separate, apart, and above the real stuff of our daily lives, but a way of looking at and coping with the personal, social, and political issues in our lives. It reminds us that prayer is the interplay of the highest we know about God and our daily struggle to make ourselves, our nation, and our world a good place in which to live."

—*Congressman Jesse L. Jackson Jr.*

"It seems that Jean Lesher has located all of the great thinkers on prayer in the world and has included their deepest thoughts on this timely subject in this magnificent new book."

—*Millard Fuller, Director, Habitat for Humanity International*

"I recommend this book to every person who quests for a deeper prayer life and for the common good in our society."

—*Monsignor John J. Egan, DePaul University, Chicago*

"This wondrous collection reflects the yearnings of humanity for a profoundly refreshed way of living together in community. The sense of human kinship runs deep among the writers of these 'prayers for the common good.' "

—*Kathleen S. Hurty, General Director, Church Women United*

"In a day when our world is too often circumscribed by individual and self-interests, Jean Lesher has brought us a richly diverse spiritual resource that points us in the other director: concern for our common life and destinies. She does this through the poignant insights of those who have lived their lives mostly in public—and always for the public good."

—*James L. Waits, Executive Director, Association of Theological Schools in the United States and Canada*

"Jean Lesher's prayers come to a world that needs them."

—*Paul Simon, Director, Public Policy Institute, Southern Illinois University at Carbondale*

"The collection breaks through the barriers of time, nation, faith, and gender with gems of discovery. These 'prayers' are a strong voice for peace, justice, and the global community. *Prayers for the Common Good* is a great resource both private and public."

—*Mary Nelson, President, Bethel New Life, Chicago*

"*Prayers for the Common Good* is an outstanding new devotional companion for those whose faith journey takes them along the road of community, justice, and service. . . . Lesher has gathered the wisdom of the ages in a fine single volume that will find usefulness in parishes, homes, and in the briefcases of the faithful wherever they travel. I recommend it highly for both corporate and individual prayer."

—*Rev. Dr. Joan Brown Campbell, General Secretary, National Council of the Churches of Christ in the USA*